Antrew Walk.

The New
How to
Advertise

Kenneth Roman and Jane Maas

**KOGAN
PAGE**

First published in the United States of America in 1976, entitled
How to Advertise. Second revised edition 1992, a Thomas Dunne
Book. Both editions published by St Martin's Press, 175 Fifth
Avenue, New York, NY 10010, USA.

First edition published in Great Britain in 1979, this edition
1992. Both editions published by Kogan Page Ltd, 120
Pentonville Road, London N1 9JN.

British Library Cataloguing in Publication Data

A CIP record for this book is available from the British Library.
ISBN 0 7494 0843 X

Printed and bound in Great Britain by Clays Ltd, St Ives plc.

For David Ogilvy,
who taught the principle
of searching for principles.

Contents

Foreword:
David Ogilvy

This was the foreword to the first edition.

I f you aspire to become a good doctor or a good lawyer, you can learn a lot by reading textbooks. But if you aspire to become a good advertising man or woman, you cannot learn from textbooks, because there aren't any good ones. So you have to learn everything on the job.

There are two things wrong with this. First, it can take half a lifetime (as in my own case). Second, you will be lucky if you can find a boss who knows enough to teach you anything.

Here, at last, is a book from which you can learn a lot about the practical business of advertising. When you have read it, you will know what it took me 25 years to learn on the job. Lucky you.

Everything in the book bears out what I have learned. It is all valid information, worth its weight in gold. Ken Roman and Jane Maas, who wrote it, know what they are talking about. From experience.

Ken is in charge of a very big advertising account, with a team of 24 executives under his command. He also understands the problems that face clients; he was once a client himself.

Jane Maas is a copywriter, and an avid student of advertising. She has made it her business to study the factors that make some campaigns succeed while others fail. And like Ken, she is uncommonly sensitive to the role of the client-agency partnership, from which all good advertising is born.

DAVID OGILVY
1976

Preface:
Principles

This book is not designed to instruct creative people how to develop advertising, nor to tell media planners how to write a media plan or researchers how to research. It is intended for people who are responsible for the entire advertising process from beginning to end, to help them manage that process effectively. While written primarily for advertisers, it talks over their shoulders to agencies as well. While practical and comprehensive, it is necessarily top-line—as experts in specific disciplines will recognize.

How to Advertise was published in 1976; in advertising, that's a lifetime ago. Almost everything in the business has changed in the intervening years—people and markets, creative strategies and production techniques, media and technologies. This new edition adds chapters and material on major issues that have emerged and are likely to increase in importance:

- The value of brands.
- Global brands, and how to move ideas around the world.
- Audience segmentation and target marketing.
- Promotion, and the shift of power to the retailer.
- Data-base marketing.

It reaches out to the smaller advertiser with a chapter on brochures and sales pieces, recognizing that the principles in the other chapters—if not the budgets—also apply to them. There is a new chapter on what it takes to succeed in an advertising business that is restructuring, plus fresh examples and case histories throughout.

What have *not* changed are the underlying principles of strategy and communications.

Creativity is a means, not an end. The purpose of advertising is to help advertisers make a profit and grow. A landmark study by the Strategic Planning Institute, an independent research organization, and the Ogilvy Center for Research & Development established convincing correlations between

- advertising expenditures and market share
- advertising expenditures and perceptions of product quality (and the price a product can command)

It pays to advertise, and the place to start is with *principles:* what works, what doesn't—and why.

As agency people, we have discovered that the biggest and best advertising ideas come about through the encouragement of a strong, knowledgeable, and enthusiastic client. So the first principle is partnership, the heart and soul of great advertising.

KENNETH ROMAN
JANE MAAS
New York, 1992

1 Brand-Building Strategies

"**B**RANDS RISE AND FALL on the strength of their advertising," says Hamish Maxwell, the former chairman of Philip Morris, the largest consumer products company in the world.

How Valuable Are Brands? "In the last three years," wrote Mr. Maxwell in 1989, "Philip Morris has bet more than $18 billion on its belief that the future of consumer-goods marketing belongs to the companies with the strongest brands. We acquired General Foods in 1985 and Kraft in 1988 for $5.6 billion and $12.9 billion, respectively, largely because their brands were successful."

Strong brands command consumer loyalty, are more resistant to price competition, and help consumers make decisions. They also have more leverage with the trade.

What Is a Brand? Another international consumer-goods giant, Unilever, starts its *Unilever Plan for Great Advertising* by talking about *brands*, not advertising:

Unilever is in the business of marketing brands, not products.

What is the difference?

A product is merely a category—a whole class of goods, e.g., cars, cameras, detergents, toothpastes, margarines.

Unilever therefore often markets several brands in one category.

A brand is more distinctive than a product. It is first of all a name, a means of identification. It is secondly a set of added values, values which offer both functional and psychological benefits to the consumer: performance in use; price; packaging; color, taste and smell; shape and form; associations; and the brand's *advertising*.

The totality of these values makes up the brand's personality, as perceived by the consumer.

Building brand equity—and selling products—is what advertising is about. Strategies are the foundation on which advertising is built.

A Blueprint for Advertising Advertising is the art of enclosing a sales proposition in an attention-getting, involving vehicle and positioning the product uniquely in the consumer's mind. Creative strategy documents differ in form and terminology, but any good one must cover:

■ **Objective:** The problem to be solved. What do you want the consumer to think or do?

■ **Target audience:** Who is your most important prospect, and what should you know about that person?

■ **Key consumer benefit:** Why should the consumer buy your product or idea?

■ **Support:** The reason for the consumer to believe. What makes you different from others who make the same claim?

■ **Tone and manner:** The projection of your product's personality.

Like a building, advertising needs a plan, a blueprint.

HOW TO BUILD A STRATEGY

First, you need facts about your brand of product or service. Study the market, the product, and the competition; understand the consumer and what needs your brand can satisfy.

Then think about the information you have gathered. Organize the facts. Develop hypotheses. Fill in gaps with missing information or conduct additional research, if necessary, to get critical answers.

At this stage, you should decide on the key opportunity for your brand—*the objective*. What do you want the consumer to think or do as a result of the advertising?

The strategic process takes someone from point A—how customers and prospects see the brand today—to point B—how you want them to see it as a result of advertising.

POINT A	POINT B
Who buys or uses the brand now (and how often)?	Whose behavior do we want to change?
Who does not use the brand? What do they use?	Do we want users to use it more, or do we want to attract nonusers (or both)?
Why?	How?

Strategy is simply the description of how the advertising will get the prospect from point A to point B.

What message will make them change attitudes and behavior?

Are we dealing with tangible product benefits, emotional benefits, or just feelings?

What is the promise? The test of a good strategy is whether what it contains, if communicated effectively in advertising, will take someone to that destination.

Developing a strategy to convince young children not to experiment with crack started with the discovery that authority figures weren't convincing; kids considered themselves smart and able to handle the drug.

An effective strategy was found: showing kids that the drug dealers were laughing at them and considered them easy marks.

Here are ten checkpoints to keep in mind as you hammer out an advertising strategy.

1. Be single-minded. The essence of positioning is sacrifice; you have to give up some points to make the important ones stand out.

While New York City has plenty of tourist attractions, the "I love New York" campaign successfully promoted tourism to New York City by its single-minded focus on Broadway theater, which research showed had the greatest appeal to visitors.

2. Make it fit an overall plan. Don't let the product, price, or package go off in one direction while the advertising goes off in another.

Everything about the Macintosh computer was designed to be simple and to be user friendly, from the products and brochures to the direct mail and advertising ("A computer for the rest of us").

3. Keep your objectives focused and reasonable. Overambition is the pitfall of most strategies. Don't try to be all things to all people or to sell a product for all occasions. Don't ask people to change deeply ingrained habits; it's much easier to get them to change brands.

4. Make your strategy easy to use. It should be very short, very sharp, and leave no room for misunderstanding. One page, with as much backup rationale as you need. If you can't get it on a page, the chances of getting it into a 30-second commercial are slim.

5. Decide where your business is going to come from. Unless you have a product that will bring new consumers into the market, your business will generally come from an existing brand or category segment.

NutraSweet was positioned as a replacement for sugar rather than against Sweet 'n Low and other artificial sweeteners, a much smaller market.

6. Make a meaningful promise to the consumer. The promise is a summary statement of the benefits of a product. It can be objective or subjective, rational or emotional, or a combination of these.

"You're in the Pepsi Generation" captured a younger audience by promising a desirable self-image as well as taste and refreshment.

"Promise, large promise, is the soul of an advertisement," said Dr. Samuel Johnson.

7. Understand the importance—or unimportance—of your product. Consumers make two kinds of decisions relating to ego involvement, points out consultant Steve Arbeit.

"A low-ego-involvement decision is one that says very little about me as an individual. Consider the brand of rice; there's not a great deal of financial risk or social risk. In spite of what advertising may tell you, your friends and family probably don't judge you by the way your rice turns out.

"A high-ego-involvement decision is one that makes a statement about me as an individual: the car I drive, maybe even the tires I use, the beer I drink. . .all those things that give some notion of how I see myself, how my choices reflect my personality or interests.

"Our objective is to raise the level of ego involvement, and to guide the consumer decision into brand loyalty."

8. Set yourself apart. Make your promise convincing. Billions of dollars have been spent behind each of six words: *new, white, cool, power, refreshing,* and *relief.* Why should the consumer believe you?

The A. C. Nielsen Company studied the introductions of hundreds of new products and concluded that the second product introduced in a market typically gains only half the share of the pioneer brand. To succeed, the second brand must either be significantly better or must spend significantly more in media.

9. Relate the unknown to the known. With a new product, you must give people a frame of reference (unless it is obvious). Tell people what it replaces, and why it is better.

> *Country Time was introduced as a convenient way to get "the taste of good old-fashioned lemonade."*

10. Keep your strategy up to date. Consumers and markets change, and you must be sensitive to this, without damaging the essence of what the brand stands for.

> *Dove beauty bar was introduced on the proposition of softer skin because it contained "one quarter cleansing cream." When sales of cleansing cream products declined, the reason-why was modified to "one quarter moisturizing cream"—and the brand rose to number one in sales dollars.*

> *Mercedes-Benz has long been positioned as "Engineered like no other car in the world." Early commercials used torture-test road demonstrations to prove performance. As consumer attitudes shifted, engineering was used to prove safety.*

The first question to be asked of any new advertisement is, "Is it on strategy?" Put your strategy statement in writing, and refer to it *every* time you review creative work.

WHY BRANDS FAIL

Brands fail for many reasons: bad products, bad research, bad pricing, bad distribution, bad luck—and bad advertising. But the reason most brands fail is bad thinking, which really means bad strategies.

The fact that you have conscientiously filled out a strategy statement does not make it right. "There's always an easy solution to every human problem," said H. L. Mencken. "Neat, plausible and wrong."

Keep these don'ts in mind:

■ *Don't lose sight of your consumer.* Most strategies focus too much on the attributes of a product, too little on the consumer, especially on consumer attitudes and usage patterns.

> *There are two kinds of cold sufferers—those who stay at home until they feel better, and those who drag themselves to work no matter how they feel. Contac users fall into the second category, leading to its positioning as "The keeps-you-going cold medicine."*

■ *Don't overrely on research.* Research is an aid to judgment; it is not the whole answer, nor is it infallible. Too often we get a research report, read only the executive summary—and accept it as truth. But numbers are subject to interpretation, which can be biased by personal points of view.

Dig into the research. Read the entire report; study the tables. Check the questionnaire to see how the questions were framed. Then decide if the conclusions lead you in the right direction.

■ *Don't belabor the obvious.* Convenience is quickly communicated and easily understood. It is much harder to communicate how good your product is; that's what the advertising should focus on.

What is obvious about frozen dinners is that they are convenient. What is important is how they taste.

■ *Don't give up the high ground.* In most categories there is one benefit more meaningful than any other—*the high ground.* It's what people ultimately buy the product for and what must be important in the advertising. In laundry detergents, it's clean; in cold medicines, it's relief.

People buy diet soft drinks in part to reduce sugar intake, or to control weight. But the reason for buying a particular brand is taste, the high ground. "Diet Coke—just for the taste of it."
Certainly brand leaders should never give up the high ground, but even small brands should think twice before opting for niche strategies.

■ *Don't use popularity as a strategy.* There's not much consumer benefit in telling people that you sell a lot of your product. Popularity of a brand is a result, not a reason-why.

■ *Don't use price as a strategy.* Few products have become long-term successes using low price as a strategy. Sooner or later, people buy quality. Products must provide true *value* to the consumer. Value is a combination of quality and price. A cheap car that falls apart in a few years is a poor value; a luxury automobile that lasts, doesn't cost much to maintain, and commands a good resale price is a good value. Quality times price equals value.

■ *Don't argue.* For categories like issue advertising, stating the facts as you see them won't change people's minds. Instead of arguing, offer information or service or some other reason to pay attention.

■ *Don't forget to offer a benefit.* People don't buy products, they buy expectation of benefits. Every year people buy one million quarter-inch drill bits—not because they want quarter-inch drill bits, but because they want quarter-inch holes.

Don't confuse attributes with benefits. Speed in a computer, for example, is an attribute; the benefit is saving time.

■ *Don't walk away from a winner.* People have ingrained attitudes about your brand. Don't let "improvements" change them; line extensions and product improvements should always make a brand *more* of what you say it is, never something less or different.

Don't change strategy easily, even when shifts in attitude or slipping sales tell you something is wrong. Problems could be the result of many factors—product, competition, market conditions. A long-term winning strategy should be the *last* thing to change, never the first.

The first thing about winning is not to lose.

QUALITY: THE SECRET INGREDIENT

Advertising works best if it is selling a product or service that is better than the competition. It is not a cosmetic to cover up deficiencies in quality.

Ford moved past General Motors in total earnings with cars based on a completely reengineered chassis, a breakthrough aerodynamic design, and a commitment to manufacturing and quality standards above any domestic competition.

TWA moved into the top three for U.S. airlines with a strategy to make traveling "hassle-free"—backed by round trip boarding passes, the first business class section, and pull-out footrests and reclining seats in first class.

The success of Procter & Gamble, who has strong brands in 20 high-volume consumer product categories, is often misattributed to more media dollars spent outadvertising the competition. But the secret of P&G's winning brands lies in a more fundamental commitment to develop and maintain superior products.

> *The key to successful marketing is superior product performance. If the consumer does not perceive any real benefits in the brand, then no amount of ingenious advertising and selling can save the brand.*
>
> ED HARNESS
> *P&G Chairman, 1977*

Once in the market, the product is continuously improved to keep it preferred versus competition. P&G management states that it does not believe in product life cycles and claims to have made 55 significant modifications in Tide in the 30 years following this brand's introduction. This confidence in their product superiority has given P&G the confidence to invest in large advertising and sampling programs.

"Advertising a bad product," said Bill Bernbach, "only makes it fail faster."

2 Television: Beating Clutter

I T'S TOUGHER EACH year to get viewers to watch your commercial. Most advertising messages are ignored. Is *anybody* watching?

Clutter is real. Mapes & Ross, a research firm, reports that 80 percent of Americans can't remember the typical commercial one day after they've seen it. That statistic shouldn't surprise. The average person is exposed to 700 advertising messages a day, and that doesn't include messages that aren't measured, from those on milk cartons to skywriting. With the remote control, viewers can "zap" commercials and turn to one of dozens—soon to be hundreds—of other channels.

Solutions come and go. The animation technique called Claymation helped make the Dancing Raisins for the California Raisin Board the most popular commercial of the mid-80s. A flock of imitators followed, and the fad was pronounced dead within five years. Other innovative production techniques, such as shaky camera testimonials, broke through the clutter for a time, then faded away.

"What drives this business is the never ending search for some new way to wake up the audience," says a director at a computer animation studio.

A sound strategy alone won't make them watch. Neither will a commercial that shouts. You must grab viewers with a meaningful strategy wrapped in a strong creative idea.

THE KEY: INVOLVEMENT

The way to get viewers to watch your commercial is to involve them, so they *want* to watch. There are several routes.

■ **Provide information they want.**

"Is it going to be scary?" asks a child going into exploratory surgery, in the opening of a General Electric commercial. It describes how that fearful process can now be performed without a scalpel, without anesthesia, even without a hospital stay—with a GE magnetic resonance imager.

■ **Present a problem to which you have the solution.**

A child who stutters is seen at a computer, saying, "S-s-s-sometimes, k-k-kids laugh when I t-talk." She goes on to type that nobody laughs when she writes. I believe I can be the best writer ever, *she types, in a John Hancock spot promoting the need for a college fund, from its "Real life, real answers" campaign.*

■ **Present a situation with which they identify.**

A young couple are on a first date in a restaurant. She reaches for the check—taking out her American Express Card. He says, "Okay, I'll get it next time." She thinks,

"Oh, great, there's a next time." Women identified with this campaign, which helped change the composition of the predominately male American Express franchise.

■ **Provide appropriate entertainment.**

Michael Jackson doesn't just perform for Pepsi; he symbolizes "the choice of a new generation."

Great advertising provides some reward for watching. It is relevant to people's needs, their interests, values, and life-styles.

HOW TO READ A STORYBOARD

The challenge is to look at a piece of paper with tiny illustrations and a few words and be able to visualize an involving, dramatic piece of film.

A commercial is presented in the form of a "storyboard" that pictures the main action of the commercial and describes what the viewer will see (the video) and hear (the audio). It will generally include some technical terms, only a few of which you must know. (See the Glossary.)

Casting and special effects are particularly hard to visualize. It helps to show clips from television shows or movies to suggest the kind of actors or actresses wanted or to demonstrate unusual production techniques. The larger issue is what to look for in a storyboard.

Does it deliver the strategy as the central idea?

If it doesn't, *turn it down.* You'll never have an easier decision. It may be the funniest storyboard you've ever seen, or the most heart-rending, but if it doesn't focus on a relevant selling idea, a central idea that is consistent with the strategy, you will be spending a lot of time and money on a commercial that will fail.

The next question: Will it involve the viewer and communicate the strategy? Here are ten principles:

1. The picture should tell the story. Forget every other point and remember this one, and you'll be ahead of the game. Too often when people look at a storyboard, their eyes shift to the words describing what the commercial will say. Television is a visual medium; that's why the people in the audience are called *viewers*. They react to and remember what they *see*.

Try this trick: cover the words. What is the message of the commercial with the sound turned off? Is there a message at all?

2. Look for a visual symbol. Here's another test you can apply to a storyboard. Can you pick out one frame that visually sums up the whole message and expresses the idea memorably?

> *A charging herd of bulls, the central idea of Merrill Lynch's "Bullish on America" campaign, was such a powerful symbol that it became the firm's logotype.*

3. Grab the viewer's attention. The first five seconds of a commercial are crucial: they will either hold the audience or lose it. Analysis of audience reaction shows either a sharp drop or sharp rise in interest with the commercial opening.

The viewer must find something immediately to *want* to keep watching. Don't count on surprise endings to save a commercial.

4. Be single-minded. Simple storyboards may fool you. They look dull on paper, but TV is a medium that thrives on simplicity. Conversely, a fascinating storyboard often translates into a busy commercial that is hard to follow.

A good commercial is uncomplicated. It never makes the viewer do a lot of mental work. It must be simple and clear.

> *A bottle of wine is set down next to a bowl of mussels, which clap their shells in applause. The wine's promise: "For food with good taste."*

Longer commercials should not add copy points. The basic commercial length in the U.S. remains 30 seconds, despite the growing popularity of :15s. Longer commercials, whether :45s or :60s, tell the same story but with more time for mood and emotion.

While there are obvious constraints with shorter messages, it is interesting how much can be packed even into a :15—demonstrations, drama, emotion. Think of them as long :10s, not as shorter :30s.

A recent study by the Association of National Advertisers indicates that :15s can be effective as reminder messages but less effective in launching something new. They also do some harm to the television environment by increasing clutter.

When your campaign includes several message lengths, look at the shortest one first. If the message cannot be delivered effectively in that time, you're not being single-minded.

5. Register the name of your product. Sometimes a viewer will remember the commercial but not the name of the product, particularly if it is a new product. Make it easy to remember.

For Bartles & Jaymes wine coolers, advertising created spokesmen Frank Bartles and Ed Jaymes, who introduce themselves in each commercial.

"Nupe it with Nuprin" registers the name of this body pain medicine.

Brand names that start with "soft" consonants—*M*s and *N*s, for example—are easier to forget that those with "hard" ones like *T*s or *K*s. That's why George Eastman invented the name Kodak for his cameras, and why names like Coke and Tide are so easy to remember.

6. People are interested in people. You'll have a more memorable commercial, and often a more persuasive one, if you show people speaking *on camera.*

A United Way spot shows a woman on camera speaking directly to the viewer: "I don't know you, but I love you." Much more powerful than showing scenes of how she was helped with her disembodied voice-over in the background.

7. Show a payoff. At some point, show that your product does what you say it will do.

When AT&T tells people to "Reach out and touch someone," it usually shows people being touched emotionally while talking on the phone.

8. Reflect your brand personality. It takes dedication and consistency to maintain a brand personality. Reject advertising that conflicts with it or takes it in a different direction.

A Lego commercial starts on one side of the screen with a mouse built of Lego pieces. On the other side is a Lego cat. The mouse quickly turns itself into a dog; the cat responds by becoming a fire-breathing dragon; the dog becomes a fire engine. . . . and so on, all reflecting Lego's fun personality.

It often helps to have a written personality statement of your product. If it were a person, what sort of individual would it be?

When people write Chevrolet advertising, they start with a written personality statement of a guy called Joe. Joe is 27 years old. He's a former Marine. He's not a genius, but a smart guy. Gregarious, a man of the people, likes girls, a family man. Works hard at his job, but <u>loves</u> sports.

9. Less is more. Don't try to jam everything into your commercial; you'll bury your most important message.

Try this discipline. When you ask for ten words to be added, identify which ten you'd delete to make room for them.

10. Build campaigns. Great advertising ideas can always be built into campaigns. They are never one-shots.

When you look at new advertising for your product or service, look for a sustainable idea. Successful advertising says the same thing over and over, with variations on a theme.

A fast way to decide if a commercial will extend into a campaign is to look at the storyboard and pretend you are going to have to write the next commercial.

WHICH DRAMATIC FORM WORKS BEST?

There are several dramatic paths, and they are timeless—some go as far back as the Bible. The parable makes a point by telling a story, as does the slice-of-life. The parting of the Red Sea is a demonstration; Job's statement of faith, a testimonial. There is Moses as presenter, with the Ten Commandments. The Bible is full of involving appeals like emotion and sex.

TV advertising uses a number of these dramatic techniques. Each has its unique strength, and one may be more appropriate than another for your brand. They are not mutually exclusive; a demonstration is frequently used in combination with a testimonial or slice-of-life.

Demonstrations: to show a product advantage.

If your product has an advantage that can be shown, *show it.* There are few stronger techniques than demonstrating that your product does what you say, or does it better than competition. Seeing is believing.

> *A French commercial for Super Glue showed a man being glued by his shoes to a ceiling and then delivering the message while hanging upside down.*

It can be simple or dramatic.

When you cannot show the real thing, consider a symbolic representation to make your point.

If you do use a demonstration, make sure it is proving a point central to your story, since—if done correctly—it will be the most memorable part of the commercial.

Testimonials: to make a point believable.

When you can't demonstrate a product advantage, consumers have to take your word for it. They might rather take the word of fellow consumers who testify that in their experience, the product does what you say it will do.

Testimonial campaigns require an idea beyond the technique. Otherwise, they are just talking heads.

Users of Dove beauty bar talk convincingly about something that cannot easily be shown—how much softer their skin feels after "the seven-day test"—using Dove instead of soap for seven days.

Testimonials say to the viewer, "This is the truth." There is an authenticity about using real people that is hard for an actor to simulate: an awkward pause, tangled syntax, a clearing of the throat, less than perfect makeup or wardrobe.

Testimonees can be ordinary men or women, or experts. They must be convincing users of the brand. A racing car driver for a motor oil typifies endorsements by experts. So does Michael Jordan for Nike or Gatorade. An expert can also be an average consumer with an above average knowledge of the product.

How does the snowplow driver get to the snowplow when there is a blizzard? Volkswagen turned the snowplow driver into an expert on which car is most reliable in bad weather.

Presenters: to symbolize the brand.

Presenters can be actors, celebrities, or created personalities. The best presenter is one who goes beyond the message and builds a strong image for the brand.

*Paul Hogan transferred his engaging Australian
"Crocodile Dundee" movie image as a spokesman for the
country.*

Research suggests that celebrities enhance attention value
and persuasion, if there is a good match between the
product or message and the celebrity.

*Bill Cosby is not just a spokesperson for Jell-O; he is Jell-O.
Like Jell-O, he is fun and wholesome—and always a kid at
heart.*

You can create a celebrity by putting the head of a company in front of a camera. However, few CEOs have the
TV presence that the spokesperson role demands.

*A notable exception: Frank Perdue for Perdue Farms ("It
takes a tough man to make a tender chicken").*

Celebrities also present risks. They can get sick, or just
get into trouble.

Slice-of-life: to involve people with the brand.

It's the oldest dramatic technique of all—actors telling a
story. A little play unfolds, allowing people to become
involved with the brand, which holds center stage. Often
it opens with a problem—to which the brand is the solution.

"Problem-solution is as old as advertising itself," points
out European creative director Luis Bassat, "simply because the basic function of many products is to solve people's problems. But avoid the temptation to make the
commercial all problem; the *solution* is what you are selling."

A powerful technique, the slice works best when it dra-
matizes real-life situations that people can identify with.

Maxwell House introduced French Roast coffee with a fresh and contemporary slice-of-life—in France. A young couple explores predawn Paris and finishes a romantic evening with coffee in a bistro.

Animation: most commonly to reach children.

Watch Saturday morning TV and you'll quickly grasp the appeal of cartoon animation for cereals, candy, toys, or any other product principally directed at children. Cartoon animation ranges from full animation to characters "rotoscoped" in combination with film, like Tony the Tiger for Kellogg's. New computer techniques are cutting the costs and time to produce both.

Cartoons can also talk to adults.

Owens-Corning Fiberglas closely links its distinctively pink fiber-glass insulation with the Pink Panther, who also appears in stores and at trade shows.

Animated characters are especially effective when used in merchandising at the retail level.

Comparative advertising: to challenge the competition.

Naming names—for example, "The Pepsi Challenge," in which Coca-Cola was shown to lose in taste tests—is an increasingly popular way to challenge established market leaders. (This is not the same as competitive advertising, in which the "other leading brand" is never named.)

Identifying competition is a high-risk technique. Research shows that viewers are often confused as to which brand is being advertised or why one brand is better than the other. With all the controversy about comparative advertising, there is one point of agreement: don't advertise your competitor if you are the market leader.

Sex and humor: in their place.

It's no news that sex sells and that jokes entertain; whether they are effective as advertising techniques depends on their relevance. Both are involving devices that present the risk of diverting attention from the product to the advertising. Humor and sex work best when they grow out of the consumer benefit rather than being used as an end in themselves.

Elizabeth Taylor is a logical and appropriate sex symbol for the fragrance bearing her name, Elizabeth Taylor's Passion.

Nynex advertising uses humor to attract attention to the yellow pages, teasing viewers to guess the categories that can be found. Actors spin, clutch their chests or throats, and fall down in agony . . . to represent "Die Casting." They make the point that if you can find anything as obscure as die casting, you can find anything in the yellow pages. "If it's out there, it's in here."

Humor wears out fast, so you will need more spots to keep your campaign fresh. Caution: everybody likes humor, but it doesn't always sell the product.

Music: to cue the viewer's feelings.

One music expert is fond of saying, "It's too bad life isn't like the movies, because without music I don't know how to feel."

Music evokes feelings—of drama, of joy, of serenity, of love, of fear.

A demonstration film to make this point showed a young woman swimming in a moonlit sea. With a background score of Debussy's La Mer, *it was romantic, almost a ballet. The same film, with the music from* Jaws, *evoked a quite different emotion.*

The same Jaws *music created a totally different feeling in a spot for Roy Rogers restaurants. Two goldfish lustfully eye their mistress's dinner—a chicken club sandwich. "Hit the music!" one fish commands, and they swim across the bowl with the ominous theme creating a chuckle—and getting attention.*

Music can be written and scored especially for the advertising or licensed from the vast classical or popular repertoire.

Great music campaigns, like "I'd like to buy the world a Coke," used original music to reflect a unique strategy for a brand.

The licensing of an old song can be effective—if it enhances the core idea—but it's almost always expensive. Copyrights run as long as 85 years, so much popular music is not in the public domain. Costs can run up to $500,000 or even $1 million, depending on usage. The least costly solution is usually stock music, but the reason it's cheap is because it's not exclusive. You might find the music you're using for your beverage is also being used for a hemorrhoid medicine.

Often the best music is music that you don't even know is there. When you see an unscored commercial, it may seem flat and lacking drama. The musical punctuation—emphasizing a car's swerve on the road, for example—tells the viewer how to feel.

Then there are nonmusical sound effects (doors slamming, crickets chirping). Combined with music, all this is called "sound design."

The costs of television production have soared for a variety of reasons—new techniques, star talent, star directors, union contracts, a raising of standards, inflation. The cost of an average national spot rose to $174,000 in 1990, according to the American Association of Advertising Agencies.

One guideline is that production should not exceed ten percent of your media budget; you want advertising dollars going into "working" media to the greatest extent possible. However, a smaller brand in a big-image category may spend considerably more, as much as a third of the media budget.

There are ways to control costs—if you understand where the money gets spent.

First, make sure the people creating the advertising know the budget limitations. Challenge them to come up with memorable ideas that don't rely on expensive extras like a celebrity presenter, elaborate sets, multiple locations, foreign settings, or special film techniques. The size of the budget doesn't have to limit creative thinking. Are you looking at a strong concept or one that relies too much on technique and production values? Ask for big ideas.

Then, allow enough time. The most costly element in TV production is overtime. Six weeks is the absolute *minimum* for producing a commercial without risking overtime: two weeks to select production companies and get bids; one week for casting, wardrobe, location or sets, approval by the networks; three weeks for filming and editing.

There are three basic areas where you will be involved:

Preproduction

Production

Postproduction

Preproduction Getting involved early is better than having regrets when you're looking at the finished product. It's understandable to ask for production to be rushed so the commercial can be screened in time for a sales meeting; just don't be surprised that it adds to the cost.

Ask the agency producer and the director to discuss the *idea*—how the storyboard will be brought to life on film or tape—so everyone shares the same vision of the commercial. Plan ahead. If you are selling snow tires, shoot when the snow is on the ground rather than traveling to the Rockies out of season.

Get multiple bids (usually from three production houses) as a frame of reference. Most expensive is not necessarily best. For a great idea, directors, especially young ones starting out, will often work for a minimum to get the spot on their reel.

Request a "shooting board," which shows scene-by-scene and shot-by-shot what is needed on the film.

How will the commercial be photographed, on film or on tape? Most commercials are shot on film for reasons of quality, then edited on tape. The image is actually etched onto the film and therefore has dimension and depth. Videotape is a magnetic process with no physical imprint; the flatter image is often used for commercials in which news or a heightened sense of reality is wanted.

Production The creative process doesn't end when the board is approved; it's never too late for a better idea.

However, one immutable law of production: *Always shoot the storyboard*. Insist that the original board be produced.

It is not acceptable to have someone say that what is shown on the storyboard won't look right or can't be done or is not needed—unless the advertiser specifically approves this shift away from the as-boarded shot.

There must be someone on the set who can make decisions on the spot. You don't want to get into a costly reshoot. One other law: Change equals increased cost. For every change, insist upon *written* authorization.

Postproduction Here almost everything can be changed, thanks to the magic of tape and the speed and accuracy of digital technology. Tape editing is faster than editing on film, and little is lost in quality.

One last point: if the commercial is not built around a strong concept, no fancy production values can save it. An expression from the theater world applies: "If it's not on the page, it's not on the stage."

With a strong concept and a well-executed commercial, you'll be able to achieve the ultimate savings—the need to make fewer commercials. Wear-out is a theoretical concept; occasionally it happens in real life, but the fact is that too much money is wasted producing unnecessary commercials. Spend your advertising dollars on the TV screen, not in the studio.

3 Research: Part of the Answer

HOW DO YOU know if your advertising is working—or that it is even saying the right thing in the first place? That's the role of research.

The ideal research sample was presented in a 1947 movie, *Magic Town*. The town was called Grandview, and it was magic for being a precise cross-section of America. Predictably, in real life there is no magic town, or any magic numbers.

The mere presence of a number often gives the illusion of certainty, yet numbers are seldom as precise as they appear and must be tempered with judgment.

When the colorful baseball manager Billy Martin joined the Oakland Athletics, research said he was controversial and should not be used in the advertising. A more insightful look at the findings suggested that Billy was the best thing they had; the "Billyball" campaign almost doubled attendance over the previous year.

What research can do is to supplement judgment, and specifically,

■ *strategic research* can help identify strategic selling ideas and define the target audience before creative work begins.

■ *ad testing* can examine individual advertisements for their ability to deliver the message.

■ *in-market research* can track the effect of a campaign over time.

STRATEGIC RESEARCH

It pays to invest more time and money up front, less on testing the finished advertising. The place to start is not, as happens too often, with the message, but with the potential consumers.

■ Who are your best prospects?

■ What do they think about your product (and your competitors')?

■ What needs and wants can your product fill; how does it fit into your prospective consumers' lives?

Defining the Target Audience Once you understand who your best prospects are and why your product appeals to them, it is easier to decide what to say.

Consumer segments, even for mass market products, are increasingly fragmenting into niches, each with its own characteristics. Most companies have considerable information available in-house to begin to isolate attractive market segments. You can also buy syndicated data services, such as Simmons or MRI. These provide demographic, product usage, and some life-style information. New geodemographic systems (PRIZM, Conquest, ClusterPlus) organize U.S. households by life-styles, which can be located by zip code and are often classified by colorful category names.

Typical PRIZM groupings include Blue Blood Estates, Urban Gold Coast, Shotguns & Pickups, and Norma Rae—ville.

Another syndicated segmentation—by attitude—is available through VALS (Values And Life-Styles), developed by The Stanford Research Institute. VALS is a means of defining segments of consumers and linking their behavior to their *values*. The VALS segmentation sorts consumers into eight different life-style types, each according to psychological attitudes, financial resources, and general outlook on life.

One important breakthrough in strategic research is *micromodeling*—building a computer model of how *individuals* make purchasing decisions on certain products and brands and predicting brand preference for each consumer under changing conditions.

If one brand of traveler's checks were easier to cash, for example, what would that do to the other brand?

Tools like computer simulation will be used more in developing strategies as the costs of computing fall.

When research money is limited, a common approach is to use syndicated sources to get a general feel for the market and to supplement this knowledge with smaller, non-quantitative research on specific questions.

Identifying the Selling Message Once you have defined the target audience, you are ready for the next step: deciding what to say.

Focus group sessions are helpful in suggesting the selling messages and language that can be used in advertising. A skilled moderator leads a dozen people chosen from your target audience, focusing on issues you select.

> *Weight Watchers learned from focus groups that dieters want to feel they are in control of their own destinies—and weights. This insight was validated, and led to "You've got it in you to get it off you."*

Take care. These groups are not totally representative of a broader population sample; they can be swayed by a strong participant or a strong moderator, and they can be misleading. *Ideas from group sessions should be validated by quantitative research.*

Quantitative research is statistically projectible; qualitative research is not. *Promise testing*, one reliable and fairly inexpensive form of quantitative research to guide strategy development, takes a number of possible benefits and asks consumers from the target audience two sets of questions:

■ Is this benefit or "promise" *important?*

■ Can the product *uniquely* fulfill the promise? (Your product may have a unique benefit, but one that is not important—like better handles on a lawn mower.) Include disguised promises from your competitors' advertising, and don't forget emotional promises as well as rational ones.

"The fabric of our lives" promise for Cotton Inc. offers an emotional benefit that leads to strong advertising.

Promise testing for Q-Tips cotton swabs led to effective advertising that portrayed an emotional benefit—"I want the very best for my baby"—as well as a rational one—"50 percent more cotton at the tip, for softness."

Promises are presented in simple statements without illustration. *Concept testing* takes the strategy development process a step further with illustrations and a description of the product. How will the product fit into a person's life? Who will use it? How should it be positioned?

AD TESTING

Too often the focus is on an individual advertisement's stopping power or recall. The purpose of testing should be principally to determine how well the advertisement communicates the strategy.

You need a range of measures to evaluate an advertisement and learn how to improve it. Which measure you use relates to the specific objectives of the advertising; resist the slavish use of one system every time.

Most money spent to test advertising goes to evaluate TV advertising, which is also the focus here, although there are systems to research advertising in print and on radio.

Communications testing helps determine whether your advertising is saying the right thing—or even saying what you think it says. Communications research is usually conducted in a forced-exposure situation. A researcher shows the finished commercial or a working version (sometimes slides with a rough track) to a sample of people who fit the audience profile. What is the commercial saying to them?

You can test rough versions of commercials in photomatic or animatic form. Communication checks can spot gross errors that can be corrected in the final commercial.

Persuasion is important if you want to change views about your product and build a strong brand image. Typically, in persuasion testing, a consumer's brand choice is determined before and after being shown advertising in a program, along with commercials for other brands in different categories.

These tests work best for new packaged-goods products, less well for established brands where the consumer holds well-developed attitudes. They are least effective for nonpackaged goods (services, durable products) where the stakes are higher.

Persuasion is not easy to measure, and many advertisers believe it is more reliable to determine a powerful strategy and test to make sure the advertising communicates it.

On-air recall testing is a measure of whether your message is stopping people and whether it's getting through. A test commercial is aired in several cities; telephone interviews 24 hours later determine how many people who watched the program remember the commercial—and what it said. But there are limitations to recall scores: they penalize emotional commercials, put a premium on people's ability to memorize or verbalize, and higher is not necessarily better.

Kimberly-Clark had one of the highest recall scores on record with a commercial for its Huggies diapers that showed people holding babies and reporting leaks with an unhappy "Uh, oh!" Sales grew slowly. A new campaign, with a respectable but lower score, showed babies who were happy because Huggies kept them dry. The brand passed Luvs and Pampers and became the category leader.

How Advertising Works Interesting diagnostic work is being done on how a commercial works. This includes studies of likability of advertising, as well as "continuous" measurements—moment-by-moment evaluations of interest as a commercial is being viewed. Research consultant Alex Biel describes another technique, *cognitive response analysis*, which looks at how consumers process information and images.

> *"It starts out by asking consumers to list all the thoughts that went through their mind while looking at the advertising. It is possible to analyze from this whether or not the consumer 'rehearsed' using the brand, whether the execution swamped the message or even evoked a counterargument—'I don't think they're half as good as the brand I'm using now.' Interestingly, the Center for Disease Control uses this technique to test commercials to fight AIDS. It may be the only copy research method that actually saves lives."*

There is a great deal of research on how advertising works that relates to how consumers behave. Consumers screen advertising; they actively seek information when the stakes are high; they find habit safe and convenient; they rarely stick to a single brand; and they are most open to persuasion in categories where satisfaction is low and involvement is high. However, no single theory explains the way all brand advertising works.

IN-MARKET RESEARCH

Beyond sales, how do consumers respond to advertising in the market, with all the pressures of real-life competition? Is the advertising building the brand?

Tracking studies continuously monitor your brand and your advertising, and your competitors' brands and their advertising, for awareness, attributes, attitudes. They provide a useful measure of whether changing attitudes or market conditions mean a campaign is no longer saying the right thing—or whether competition is doing something better. A tracking study can also evaluate a new campaign. There are controlled versions of tracking studies, like Ad-tel. These use cable TV feeds and matched markets to measure in-store sales movement.

It takes a long time for brand advertising to work on people—or to wear out. Don't get impatient if sales don't take off instantly.

> *One of the most successful beer campaigns ever almost came off the air prematurely. "Miller Time," for Miller High Life, ran at heavy levels for eight months before there was a blip in sales, then continued for eight years as Miller moved up from number 13 to number two, behind Budweiser.*

Don't walk away from a successful long-running campaign just because you think it's time for a change—or because you're bored with it. Consumers may just be starting to respond to it.

GOOD RESEARCH IMPROVES THE ODDS

Here are ten principles that can improve your chance of getting reliable information:

1. Define success in advance. Establish action standards up front, against which the advertising will be evaluated. Give the researcher a clear description of the problem to be solved, not the way you think it should be done. What are you trying to find out?

2. Get the right sample. Conduct testing among prime prospects for your product. Don't neglect current users; include them in the target audience.

3. Use the appropriate interview technique. Telephone interviews are fine for short questionnaires (up to 20 minutes). One-to-one interviews are more expensive but best for conducting longer interviews and probing for in-depth understanding. Mail surveys cost the least but must be validated with a survey of nonrespondents. People who fill out questionnaires may be different from people who don't.

4. Test in the right programming. Different environments can produce different scores. Choose the kind of shows that are appropriate for your advertising; use the same program if you're testing two commercials.

5. Test the most representative message length. Don't test a 30-second commercial if :15s are the primary unit in your media plan (:30s seldom score twice as well as :15s but may have other values).

6. Test alternatives. You may be surprised to find the sure winner loses to another approach. Force yourself to look at other solutions.

7. Make sure the advertising is the only thing that changes. This is not the time to try a new package, a new price, or a new spending level. Control all variables other than the advertising, or you'll never know what the advertisement contributed.

8. Remember that people buy products, not advertising. Make sure they react as consumers, not as experts on advertising.

> *When asked which campaigns they most disliked, consumers convicted Mr. Whipple, the store manager who squeezed the Charmin toilet tissue because it was so soft. Charmin may not have been popular advertising, but it was number one in sales.*

Don't ask people their opinion about your advertising; get their reaction to the *brand*. Disguise the purpose of the interview and the identity of the advertiser sponsoring the research.

9. Be careful with numbers. Remember that the score is an approximation, and its reliability depends on the size of the sample. Ask how large a numerical difference indicates a statistical difference in the score. Another dimension of reliability is the confidence level: a 90-percent confidence level means that in nine out of ten times the results will be the same.

10. Go beyond the numbers. Pay attention not just to scores but also to rich diagnostic information like verbatim comments. These can give you clues as to how people react and why. What does the research say about the strengths and weaknesses of the idea you're testing?

There is no formula for truly superior advertising. If you use "learning" from advertising tests as a prescription for creative work, it may lead to above-average recall or persuasion scores—and mediocre advertising.

THERE'S NO SUBSTITUTE FOR JUDGMENT

In the final analysis, you can't rely totally on the numbers. They must be interpreted and understood in their full dimension, along with other information.

Use common sense. Sometimes the data just doesn't square with reality, or people may not be willing to tell the truth.

When the New York Daily News *was the newspaper with the largest circulation in the U.S., readership surveys curiously showed it being outsold by the* New York Times. *More people claimed to read the more prestigious paper. When asked a new question, "What* other *paper might you have picked up on the subway?" the correct ranking of the mass-market* Daily News *emerged.*

Research is one part of the answer; judgment is the other part.

4 Print: Selective

TELEVISION HASN'T REPLACED reading, as some people predicted; it has changed *what* we read.

Most mass magazines have departed, and there are fewer daily newspapers. But the average American is now buying more magazines each year, rather than fewer. There are thousands of magazines in print; 1.3 new titles are launched *every day*.

While daily newspapers are down, Sunday newspapers are up. They've doubled in number—and gained in weight. There are fewer big-city newspapers, but more weekly community papers and more ethnic newspapers.

What all these growing print media have in common is *selectivity*.

The great opportunity print provides is the ability to reach an audience that has a special interest in the publication and is likely to be paying close attention. Readers expect information in print; they accept and even seek out ads as part of the medium, as retailers and publishers of fashion magazines know. But readers can also easily turn the page.

Magazines: An Editorial Environment Successful editors judge the effectiveness of their work by magazine renewal rates. Three magazines with renewal rates among the highest in the business—*Good Housekeeping, Victoria*, and *Country Living*—are all under the editorial guidance of John Mack Carter. When asked his secret, John Mack responds that they are all *emotionally involving to the reader*. His editors listen carefully to the audience and respond with articles that speak to their interests. A good clue for advertisers.

Newspapers: A News Environment Headline your news with impact.

> *Within days of the overthrow of communism in the Soviet Union, Stolichnaya vodka was in newspapers with a full-page ad under the headline "We're prouder than ever to be Russian."*

The stopping power of a full-page newspaper advertisement is dramatic, but size alone will not carry the day. The difference is in the reading environment. Newspapers are retail and local, so talk to the reader in those terms.

WHAT WORKS BEST IN PRINT

It's easier to react to a print layout than a TV storyboard. The layout resembles what will appear in the publication: there will be a rough headline, a sketch of the illustration, some typed copy, and it will probably be the same size. It's equally easy to react to the wrong part of the advertisement—to get involved with words in the copy or headline and miss the point.

React to the net impression of the entire advertisement.

What is the total message at first glance? Does it clearly deliver the strategy? Will it stand out, and will it select your prospects?

Here are some fundamental principles for print advertising:

1. Use simple layouts. Avoid cluttered pages, multiple typefaces, lots of little pictures.

> *Advertisements for Hush Puppies shoes are posterlike in simplicity. A basset hound with ears blown back by an electric fan illustrates "Ventilated Hush Puppies." "Sophisticated Hush Puppies" shows the dog waiting expectantly as his water bowl is filled with Perrier.*

Your layout should follow a natural order, which is not necessarily from top to bottom. The reader's eye will go first to the most powerful element on the page.

2. The illustration is usually more important than the headline. In fashion advertising, the body copy—and occasionally even the headline—is disappearing. An evocative illustration can deliver a clear message, with no copy needed except the brand name. Sometimes a unique product or package can serve as the illustration and brand the advertisement.

> *Absolut vodka made its unique bottle into a successful campaign by turning its shape into a variety of images, from a California swimming pool to New York's Central Park.*

3. Look for story appeal in the illustration. Find something that makes the reader ask, "What's going on here?", like the man with the eyepatch who established Hathaway shirts. There's nothing inherently interesting in product-as-hero—unless it's done with a twist.

> *The scene in Paco Rabanne cologne advertising is always a barely dressed man talking on the phone to an unseen woman. The carefully staged photographs border on fantasy—an artist's loft, the cabin of a yacht, a well-furnished bachelor pad.*

4. Photographs work better than artwork. Research shows that photography increases recall an average of 26 percent over artwork. It is always preferable to artwork when showing food. Showing the completed dish has more appetite appeal than raw ingredients.

> *Mouth-watering photographs of cookies, cakes, and bread testify to Pepperidge Farm's promise of old-fashioned goodness.*

Photos help readers see how a product can be used, by whom, and when. They offer compelling visual evidence.

> *Print advertisements for the Boston Whaler showed three fishermen together in the boat. On second glance, the reader sees that the boat has been sawed in thirds and that each man is floating safely in a separate section, convincing visual argument for the boat's safety claim.*

Before-and-after or with-and-without photographs make a point more effectively than words. That's why makeover cosmetic feature stories work so well in magazines.

Put a caption under the photo; picture captions get twice as much readership as body copy. The picture with caption can almost be an advertisement unto itself.

5. Offer a benefit in the headline. The world's best-read magazine, *Reader's Digest*, has three guiding principles for headlines: present a benefit to the reader, make the benefit quickly apparent, make it easy to get.

Sports fans "get the feeling" of being there with involving photos and editorial in Sports Illustrated.

The copywriter John Caples observed, "Headlines make ads work. The best headlines appeal to people's self-interest or give news. Long headlines that say something out-pull short headlines that say nothing. Remember that every headline has one job: it must stop the reader with a believable promise."

Use the headline to select your prospect. Inject news into the headline; your product will only be new once. Localize or personalize the headline if possible.

6. Don't be afraid of long copy. Few readers stay with the average advertisement long enough to read all the way through, so don't count on the copy to carry the day. But for considered purchases that involve investing substantial time or money (a car, a vacation, a computer, for example), you o ·n can't give people too much information.

The British Tourist Authority attracts visitors with advertisements that are packed with facts, from what it costs to watch the Changing of the Guard (nothing) to the cost of a good meal in a pub (under $5.00).

Don't pad the copy with empty phrases; people are hungry for facts. Avoid manufacturer talk, and speak in plain English. And don't crowd long copy into a layout not intended to hold it. It must be designed so that the copy will be read. Long copy ads are almost a "visual" element in themselves.

7. Make it easy to read. Study newspapers and magazines; use them as models. They use classic typefaces, and not too many different ones on a page. They use capitals and lower-case letters rather than all caps, especially in text. They use serif type, like the type in this book, rather than sans serif, which looks like this. They seldom print type in reverse on a dark background, nor do they print over tones or tints or on photographs. They encourage reading by designing copy that's easy to read.

8. Every advertisement should be a complete sale. Develop an identifiable format, and make every advertisement part of a campaign. It can double recognition of your brand.

Don't assume the reader will read every ad, or even more than one. The basic proposition should be presented in its entirety every time; the campaign plays variations on a theme.

> Rolling Stone *magazine contrasts its 1960s countercultural cliché image with its surprisingly mainstream readership. A typical advertisement shows a furry little mouse under the headline "Perception" on one page; on the facing page, a computer mouse under the headline "Reality." The symbols vary; the message never does.*

9. Break out of the mold. Print can do things that television cannot; it can deliver samples, or let people sniff a fragrance. Absolut has been as creative in its form as its content. Its Christmas advertisements have pioneered such techniques as a microchip embedded on a page to deliver a holiday song, a globe filled with plastic snowflakes, and a specially designed handkerchief in an insert that appears to be a gift-wrapped package ("Open for an Absolut Surprise").

It can deliver vastly more information in the form of booklets.

Through service stations and magazines the "Come to Shell for answers" campaign delivered over one billion booklets providing automotive and other energy advice.

Print can deliver impact in small doses, with small ads run on consecutive pages, or in blockbuster inserts.

Calvin Klein sponsored an "outsert," a 116-page supplement delivered in a plastic bag with Vanity Fair. *The purpose was more than size and impact: the book form used photographs to portray an attitude rather than a product.*

Print can be as creative in its form as in its content.

10. Design the advertisement for the medium. Size makes a difference. Don't take an advertisement designed for *Life*, for example, and just reduce it for *Reader's Digest*. It must be redesigned specifically for the smaller magazine, using cropped photos to suggest what appears in the larger units.

Editorial content varies from magazine to magazine, so that should also be taken into account. Newsmagazines might suggest one approach, service books another.

There's a vast difference, too, between paper stocks. The subtle colors that can be reproduced in a fashion magazine printed on a coated stock are one thing; what will reproduce well on uncoated newspaper stock is another. You must plan for publications that offer less definition or less color.

Look at the advertisement in context, not just mounted for presentation. Ask that it be pasted up in the publication.

HOW TO CONTROL PRINT PRODUCTION COSTS

Production is going electronic, which enables advertisements to be produced more quickly and allows for roughs that are closer to the finished product. But more than technology is needed to control costs:

■ *Don't approve anything for production unless you understand exactly what's going to happen and what it will cost.*

■ *The sooner you speak up, the better—and the less it will cost.*

An expensive photographer, exotic location or elaborate set construction, night or weekend shooting, use of children or animals, special visual effects—all add costs, just as they do in the production of a TV commercial. Therefore, it is mandatory that you approve a production estimate *in advance*, before any money is committed. Get several bids on the key elements.

Agree on how you will use the artwork. A photograph for a print advertisement is bought only for a specified run, unless you agree with the photographer on a buyout. If you want to use more than one photo from the shoot or to use photos for other purposes (such as promotion), that must be negotiated.

Reading is active. You have to turn pages, focus on symbols, convert them to thoughts and ideas. Reading takes energy, attentiveness, and absorption. Readers are therefore highly selective about the advertisements they choose to read.

5 Radio and Out-of-home

WHILE IT MAY seem surprising to talk about these two media together, radio and outdoor have several important things in common. They both talk chiefly to an audience on the move. Both can deliver a large number of impressions even with limited dollars. Both are local and targeted.

The similarities stop there.

Radio is the ultimate *one-to-one* medium.

Out-of-home (of which outdoor is the most familiar) talks to large numbers of people at the same time, for the most part in *quick takes*. It includes everything from blimps to bus stop shelters, messages on clock displays and on benches, posters outside and inside buses, trains, and taxis, printed or painted outdoor boards. None of these depend on the audience to take the initiative—the medium is simply there.

Before you create advertising for either radio or out-of-home, form a mental picture of what your audience is doing when they receive the message. They are almost always doing something else at the same time.

RADIO: THE ONE-TO-ONE MEDIUM

Think about radio and the way people listen to it, each in his or her own private world. The media philosopher Marshall McLuhan observed:

> *"Radio affects people intimately, person to person, offering a world of unspoken communication between writer-speaker and the listener. A private experience."*

Radio is ubiquitous; it's *everywhere*. It's the first thing we hear in the morning, as we catch up on the news while dressing. It's with us in the car; we listen on a headset while jogging or walking to work.

We typically listen to a radio three hours a day, but we're not all listening to the same thing. Programming manuals list over 140 different program types. All-news, all-sports, Top 40 rock music, classical, country—22 types of country music alone: American country, modern country, bluegrass, progressive country, and so on. FM tends to reach the younger music listener; AM stations have become the forum for talk and information radio, with a distinctly older skew. Talk programs appeal to audiences with special interests, from gardening to investing to sex advice.

Radio is the biggest teen medium, especially in the evening and in summertime.

There are stations for ethnic and racial groups and for many nationalities—one station in Detroit broadcasts programs in 21 different languages.

You can target by time of day or by weather conditions. You can select the listener and talk one-to-one.

Some principles of radio advertising:

1. Talk one-to-one. Motel 6 talks with empathy directly to the business traveler or vacationer who is interested only in a no-frills room for the night.

> *"Hi, Tom Bodett here for Motel 6. . . . You won't get the same atmosphere as in Uncle Bruce's knotty pine rec room, but your eyes will be closed, so who cares? . . . Hey, with the money you save, you can pick up that slag glass sculpture for the mantel. It may look like a rock to your friends, but you know it's art."*

Every spot ends with the friendly line, "We'll leave the light on for you."

2. Think about the program environment. The same commercial can be more or less effective when heard in different contexts. There are differences between music formats, rock or popular or classical, between straight news and a brassy morning personality like Don Imus in New York.

3. Focus on one idea. With no pictures to rivet them, listeners are easily distracted. Be direct and clear.

> *A commercial for Sony audio tape gives each musical instrument a corresponding color—blue for saxophone, yellow for trumpet, red for drums—and concludes, "Sony Tape: full-color sound."*

4. Don't splinter your efforts. If radio is supporting your television advertising, consider using some elements of your TV campaign, especially music. While the radio advertising will be different in format, it should not be different in strategy.

5. Stretch the listener's imagination. Voices and sounds can evoke pictures, create atmosphere, transport people to wherever you want them to go.

> *The sound of a crying baby and a man's voice saying, "I'll get up this time," evokes a recognizable family situation and targets prospects for a savings bank's liquid investment accounts for young families.*

The Radio Advertising Bureau promoted the power of sound with the slogan, "I saw it on radio."

6. Make it topical. Radio commercials are relatively inexpensive and quick to produce. Take advantage of this by being topical and relevant to the season, time of day, station format, and listeners. If it's near April 15, offer tax advice. If it's cold outside, sell hot beverages or antifreeze. If it's Friday, suggest what to pick up for the weekend. If it's morning, sell coffee to get listeners going. ("The best part of waking up is Folger's in your cup.")

> *During the hay fever season, Contac tied its advertising to the pollen count in two ways: special commercials talking to allergy sufferers and a plan that increased the number of spots as the pollen count rose.*

Drive time is an obvious opportunity to talk about cars, transmissions, and automotive services like cellular phones. Researchers find that drivers remember a commercial message better than listeners at home.

7. Register your brand name. They can't see it, so be sure that they hear it.

Comics Stiller and Meara created a brand image for Blue Nun wine with a campaign of humorous commercials that played on the brand name and registered it indelibly.

8. Use the strength of music. Music evokes feelings and emotions without pictures. You can use the track from your TV commecial or something created just for radio. Be certain people can hear what's being sung. Keep the melody and lyrics simple.

9. Advertise promotions. Radio is perfect for retail advertising and promotions for national brands as well as local stores. "This week *only*" works.

Consider live-delivery commercials—scripts read by the program host—to capitalize on the announcer's credibility and personality. The price is right: no production cost. But there's a difference between reading a commercial and *delivering* a commercial.

Open Pit barbecue sauce enhanced its traditional Memorial Day and Labor Day promotions with live-delivery commercials. Each station was given a standard script, a fact sheet from which the disc jockey could improvise—and a color TV was given as a prize for the best commercial.

10. Listen to the commercial in context. Most listeners will not hear your commercial through a powerful studio audio system, nor will they be paying rapt attention. Listen to a tape in your own car, knowing that people in the listening audience will be driving or reading or talking rather than just listening.

Outdoor billboards or posters are a quick-take medium. Transit advertising (inside buses or subways) is just the opposite. The average ride is 22.7 minutes, says the Transit Advertising Association; travelers often have nothing to do but study your message. Outdoor advertising and transit advertising reach two very different audiences.

The bigger challenge is the outdoor board. It is a controversial medium. For some, it disfigures our environment and should be banned. Others deplore heavy usage by tobacco and liquor companies.

Use of outdoor boards by tobacco and liquor advertisers is actually declining, while it is on the rise for retailers, business products and automotive. Packaged goods, fashion and Hollywood are discovering the power of outdoor. The Outdoor Advertising Association has recommended that its members cut back billboards near schools and churches promoting products that can't be sold to minors.

Used with taste and common sense, outdoor is a legitimate medium that can enhance the environment. In Europe, where many artists start their careers designing posters, outdoor is viewed as a mark of civilization.

Outdoor advertising is seen by many people, it can be very local, it can pack enormous impact. Posters have to grab attention quickly and communicate *instantly*. To simulate the speed of registration, researchers use a *tachistoscope*, or T-scope, which exposes a small version of the board for seconds only.

Here are some things you can do to make sure that your board registers in seconds:

1. Keep it simple. Posters are the art of brevity. Cut out all extraneous words and pictures; concentrate on essentials.

The best billboards are nonverbal, confirms a Research International study.

Evian boards need no words to explain the visual of a fish leaping eagerly from its bowl into a glass of Evian water.

Make it digestible and easy to understand. Only one picture, and no more than seven words of copy, preferably fewer.

2. Look for a big idea. Outdoor is a bold medium; you need a poster that delivers the idea quickly and memorably. Size only magnifies dullness.

A Reebok poster shows a triumphant greyhound holding a decoy rabbit gently in its mouth. The dog is wearing Reeboks.

3. Make it stand out. Use high-impact graphics and bold lettering. The outdoor companies advise strong silhouettes and photographs cropped and enlarged to heroic proportions.

Copy must be at least 12 inches high to be read at 400 feet. Avoid special typefaces, such as script.

4. Use color to get it read. Black on yellow is the most visible combination, but other primary colors can get attention.

Campbell's soup laid the familiar red-and-white can on its side and turned it into a radiator, with the headline "Red and White for the Winter Blues."

Use daylight fluorescent color with care. It increases impact and visibility but also creates a circus effect.

5. Localize. Geography can present a unique opportunity:

*Drivers coming through New York's Midtown Tunnel are
greeted by a board for Bud Light beer: "The light at the
end of the tunnel."*

Tailor language to ethnic neighborhoods for all the obvious reasons. Localized posters—"New in Chicago"—are
practical, even in short runs. You can also mention a
specific location or dealer.

6. Look for human, emotional content. Here's one medium
where humor works. It appeals to bored travelers and
can increase memorability.

*"Exactly how mad is she?" asks the headline. The visual is
three flower arrangements—small, medium, and large—on
an American Floral Marketing Council poster.*

7. Announce news. You can reach 100 percent of a market
in the first day, according to Nielsen. For instance, 500
carefully placed posters in Los Angeles will be seen by
virtually every prospect the day they go up.

Don't overlook the impact on the trade. The local supermarket manager may never see your commercials on
TV but will notice a big poster across the street from the
store.

8. Use all dimensions. You're not limited to a flat, rectan-
gular poster (although that is the least expensive). Consider breaking out of the borders to underline the
message.

*J&B Scotch literally turns down the upper corner of a
board to go with the line, "Curl up with a J&B."*

9. Think direct marketing. More direct-response advertisers are using outdoor. Consider recruiting prospects for

your product or service. Some advertisers find that an 800 number on a board generates more response than other media. It helps to give consumers words they can associate with the product—like 800-OK-CABLE—instead of pure numbers.

10. Extend your campaign. Outdoor advertising is ideal to remind people of brands, brand images, and brand positioning.

The Marlboro campaign has been so strong and consistent over so many years that boards can occasionally show only the cowboy, without the package or brand name.

HOW TO CONTROL OUTDOOR COSTS

Location, location, location are the first three real estate principles. Billboards cost more in high-traffic locations— $10,000 or more per month on Sunset Boulevard, considerably less farther out.

Technology has advanced on this front as in other print media with computer image reproduction. Posters that were once called "30-sheets" are no longer made up of 30 large printed sheets of paper. Fewer sheets are now used, but the term remains to designate size. The standard size for most boards is 12 feet by 24 feet. Most large boards can now be printed, so it doesn't make much sense to have them painted unless your posting is 10 boards or less. Overlays, called "snipes," can add or change copy, list a local dealer, or announce a new date or address.

The key to controlling production costs is budgeting time. Allow four to five weeks to print four-color boards or you will run up overtime costs. Add at least a week for shipping and 10 days more prior to posting. For painted boards, allow 45 days.

It's a curious paradox that strong posters continue to be created for a medium that is not growing, while at the same time, there are all too few standout commercials on radio, a medium that is expanding. The moral: advertisers should sustain outdoor as an advertising medium with creative work that is distinctive (and enhances the environment)—and grab the radio opportunity with commercials better tuned to the listener.

6 Direct Marketing: Accountable

THE JOY OF direct marketing is its account-ability: you quickly know the exact results of an advertising investment. The fastest-growing communications discipline, direct has been driven by several minirevolutions, including

- sophisticated computer models and better lists
- the convenience of credit cards and the 800 telephone number
- dual income households and other changes in lifestyles and shopping habits

Direct marketing is defined by direct marketing expert and author Drayton Bird as "any activity whereby you communicate directly with your prospect or customer and he or she responds directly to you." The ability to market directly to an individual or business with increasing precision has resulted in explosive growth. New analytical tools have created proprietary data bases, mailing lists enriched with information about an individual or family *beyond* the address. Data-base direct marketing takes the medium to a new level by increasing the ability to match a product and message with a person's proclivity to buy. "It's as important to reach the right people as it is to reach lots of people," reports *Business Week* of how data bases have changed advertisers' thinking.

IT PAYS TO TEST

The secret of successful direct marketing is knowing what has worked, and challenging those results with new testing every time.

> *"We learn the principles and prove them by repeated tests. This is done through keyed advertising, by traced returns, largely by the use of coupons. We compare one way with many others, backward and forward, and record the results. When one method invariably proves best, that method becomes a fixed principle."*

So wrote Claude Hopkins, the most successful copywriter of his era, in *Scientific Advertising* in 1923.

It is common to find that one mailing will produce many times the response of another for the *same* product.

> *A series of tests for a shoppers buying service included mailings to 12 lists, three prices, two ways to pay, different times for mailing, alternative ways to respond, and several creative approaches. The best combination of all these factors pulled 58 times better than the worst combination.*

You don't have to be big to test. In many cases, if you can generate 100 to 200 responses—enough for a statistically valid sample—you can get away with mailing as few as 10,000 pieces.

Don't assume *anything*. You will be surprised.

■ People will read long letters—they often pull better than short ones.

■ Some months (or even weeks or days) are more productive than others.

■ Sometimes a higher price will produce more response than a lower one.

■ People will respond again and again to the same mailing. Never change a successful mailing until you have a *proven* winner to replace it.

It always pays to test if you plan to mail to a substantial number of people, or if you plan to mail more than once.

Test. Test anything that could significantly increase response rates or decrease promotional costs: copy, layout, colors, offers, terms, prices, premiums, mailing lists, enclosures, the complete package. Even fractional improvements year after year can make a substantive difference in profitability. But don't test minutiae; be selective.

Test only one variable at a time. If you test several, you won't know which helped, or how much. Then combine all your winners and test again.

If you cannot test, take advantage of the testing of others. When you receive the same mailing over and over, year after year, you can be reasonably sure it has been proven in testing.

THE TRUE-VALUE CONCEPT

To decide how much to invest in each potential customer, you must know or estimate how much each customer is worth. It will almost always cost more to get a new customer than you will receive in an initial order. If you expect people to order something just once, the calculation is easy: will you get enough money to cover the cost of the mailing package plus the cost of the merchandise and still make a profit?

Most direct mail is in a different category; it goes to people who may buy more than once. The object therefore is to get profitable *names*.

The New York Red Cross found that it paid to send first-time givers a free first-aid manual to convert them to donors, who were found to give in four of the following seven years, and increased their donations 20 percent.

Increasingly, mass media advertising is being used as a means to generate names for direct marketing. The key, according to John Groman of Epsilon, is that repeat customers have a measurable long-term, ongoing value. He quotes the direct marketing axiom that "it's far, far easier to sell something to the customer you have than to sell to a new customer."

The basis for evaluation is cost efficiency against a marketing objective: not just the response rate, but the cost per inquiry; not just the number of responses, but the conversion rate from inquiry to sale. If you use only efficiency as the basis for all evaluation, you will end with the cheapest mailing packages, not necessarily the most effective.

WHAT WORKS BEST IN DIRECT MAIL

With the caveats that one should assume nothing and that everything must be tested, here are some principles for effective direct mail:

1. Get to the point quickly. Much direct mail is read over a wastebasket.

Open with a message that speaks to the reader in a very personal way:

> *"Quite frankly, the American Express Card is not for everyone. And not everyone who applies for Card-membership is approved." This was the opening for a long-running mailing that beat all alternates in attracting new applications.*

"Good direct mail flatters, intrigues, charms, cajoles," says Drayton Bird, "but, above all, it gets to the point quickly, with news of benefits for the prospects."

2. Make sure the offer is right. Other than the list itself, no element will make more of a difference than what you offer the consumer in terms of product, price, or premium.

> The Economist *magazine offered subscribers three alternate renewal offers:*
>
> *$65.00 for 56 weeks*
> *$42.50 for 39 weeks*
> *$29.95 for 39 weeks*
>
> *Not surprisingly, the lowest price attracted the most subscribers. It also resulted in more conversions to full-price*

renewals and therefore the largest profit, despite the initial 40-percent reduction.

Free is the most powerful offer you can make, but beware of attracting only one-time buyers.

3. Make the envelope work for you.

It was hard not to open an envelope with a cartoon captioned "I can't take all the credit but it was my decision to hire Kenneth Roman." The cartoon showed an executive with a sharply rising sales graph and introduced a special subscription offer from the Harvard Business Review.

The envelope is what people see first. Tease them. Tip your offer. Tell them about a gift inside, or about valuable information.

"Hurrah! Hurrah! London double miles extended to August 31" is the envelope opener for United Airlines.

4. Include a letter.
If you can afford only a brochure or a letter, send the letter. It will work better for you.

Don't be afraid of long copy. Most professionals believe that a letter should always be long—and that each additional page lifts the response rate.

Make it visually interesting. Help the reader with crossheads (like "Include a letter"—above), handwritten readouts, inset paragraphs (as the Gevalia example—below).

5. Make sure the product is positioned correctly.
A promise test can help decide the best positioning.

Gevalia coffee was positioned as the choice of real coffee lovers, imported from Sweden, where people drink more coffee than anywhere else in the world.

6. Ask for the order. Don't let the prospects off the hook. Leave them with something to do, so they don't procrastinate.

Some direct marketers believe in involvement devices like yes/no tokens. More useful are tangible reasons for action, like limited-time offers or some reward for replying quickly.

Don't forget to use the P.S. It is one of the best-read parts of the letter.

7. Cultivate an appropriate brand personality. A good letter is appropriate to both the product and the audience.

> *A long-running letter from* The Wall Street Journal *talked about the 25th college reunion of two men who were very much alike and had gone to work for the same company. "But there was a difference. One of the men was manager of a small department of that company. The other was its president."*
>
> *The letter asks "What made the difference?" It doesn't say that* The Wall Street Journal *was the secret, but it does say, "The difference lies in what each person knows and how he or she makes use of that knowledge."*

Match the tone to the target audience and the subject.

8. Treat the customer as a friend. Don't resell a product to someone who is already using it. Maintain a consistent posture in treating the customer as a friend and in nurturing that relationship.

> *Taking friendship one step further, Jack Daniel's invited its best customers to become members of a club. It gave each of them one square foot of land in Tennessee, solemnly*

pronounced them Tennessee Squires, and proceeded to treat them like major landowners, who would be interested in farm equipment auctions, plans for building outhouses, or even reports of poachers on their land.

A renewal letter should assume the customer likes the product and only needs a reminder. It can convey a sense of urgency or use a special offer as an incentive.

9. Integrate direct mail with other communications. Maintain a common strategy and brand personality with everything that touches the consumer. When American Express changes a campaign or launches a new promotion, everything is integrated down to the "Take One" applications found in restaurants.

Mercedes-Benz introduced its new S-Class line with media advertising and a mailing to 100,000 owners. An eight-minute videotape showed the S-Class in action, highlighted its advancements in performance, comfort, safety and reliability, and expanded the viewer's understanding of the new line.

10. Repeat your winners. The most effective letter—your control—is the standard. Try to beat it by adding something or modifying the offer. Or "downtest"—remove elements, such as a brochure, or find other ways to save money. Test every variable, but keep using the original until you find something better, and then make that your new control.

DATA-BASE MARKETING

The strategic use of customer information has two major thrusts. It reduces advertising waste by targeting marketing efforts to high value prospects. It maximizes the value of each customer by building a relationship through continuous communications.

Contemporary direct marketing, says industry pioneer Lester Wunderman, is relationship marketing.

"What we are selling are not products, or even services, but ongoing relationships between suppliers of services or products and their individual users. Relationships require a dialogue. They can't exist without one."

The foundation of relationship marketing is the data base. The data base is simply a list of best prospects created by combining information from several sources to put attitudes and usage together with addresses and standard demographic information. Lists can be compiled from several sources, exchanged with other companies that have similar profiles, or rented from list brokers.

With powerful information like this, a company can stay close to the customer. An integrated data-base program builds profitable relationships by continually updating information from customers and building it back into personalized messages or products.

Compaq sent a letter to prospects that said, "If you're looking for a new computer, tell us which brand and model." With this information in hand, Compaq was able to send a mailing that compared the computer each person was thinking of buying with the new Compaq.

Tracking attitudes, sales, and brand loyalty leads to the concept of using a timed sequence to build unique buyer-seller relationships.

A direct marketing program for Huggies disposable diapers targeted pregnant women, sending them informational mailings before their children were born, followed by timed mailings as the babies entered different stages of development (and diaper usage).

Targeted relationship marketing.

BROADCAST ADVERTISING

Direct-response advertising on television or radio has its own unique disciplines. People are most familiar with it in the form of those long commercials on late night TV.

Broadcast direct marketers have learned the following:

■ Commercials should be as long as it takes to make the sale, often as long as the two-minute maximum. Few viewers can make a buying decision in less time than that. Also, it takes time—as much as 30 seconds—to register the response number or ordering details.

■ The best commercials set forth a problem, include a demonstration that shows why the product is the best solution, offer a money-back guarantee, and give the price.

■ There must be a sense of urgency, an offer or other reason to buy *now*: "Exclusive—not available elsewhere."

Ryder built its share of the truck rental business with two-minute commercials that raised awareness of its expertise in this market. It offered do-it-yourselfers a step-by-step moving guide, a 10-percent discount on moving supplies, and a free Sony FM Walkman radio for responders who rented a Ryder truck.

TV and radio direct response help close sales, generate leads, or supplement advertising in other media.

TELEMARKETING

There are two telephone systems in direct marketing, inbound and outbound.

Inbound is the growing use of 800 (toll-free) numbers for placing an order from an advertisement or catalogue and 900 (toll) numbers for buying a service—weather information, sweepstakes tickets, free order samples.

> *WATS Telemarketing was an integral part of the Ryder Truck Rental program. Calls generated a data base of 150,000 prospective movers and their planned moving dates.*

Outbound is the use of the phone to close a sale or offer a product or service; at its irritating worst, cold-calling is a controversial medium that is now beginning to regulate itself and limit both the hours calls are made and the tone of the call.

The voice on the telephone (and the script) is the closest thing to being in a store. On the phone, real people create the brand's image. With a well-trained staff and some self-restraint, telemarketing can be an effective and cost-efficient means of reaching people not reached elsewhere.

BUILD TRUST

Nobody—including the mailer—wants junk mail. However, one person's junk is another's passion. Some people cannot get enough garden catalogs or cookbooks or whatever. Junk mail is mail that is inappropriate—because it is addressing the wrong person, arriving at the wrong time, or using the wrong tone.

People want direct mail. They read it and they save it—if the product or service is something they *want* and if they *trust* the mailer. Research in five countries by Ogilvy & Mather Direct, the world's largest direct marketing agency, showed that the single most important thing that can be done to increase sales is to convince prospects that they can trust you. The more people trust you, the more they will buy from you.

7 Campaigns That Build Businesses

THINK OF ANY successful brand. You can almost always call to mind the advertising that helped build it:

■ "The Pepsi Generation," which created a solid position for the brand among a younger audience and made Coca-Cola seem almost old-fashioned.

■ "You deserve a break today, at McDonald's," the campaign that created a new family eating style in America and around the world.

■ The retired athletes' argument: "Tastes great." "Less filling." It ran for 17 years and made Miller Lite the second-largest-selling beer.

■ Engineering facts and performance demonstrations that proved Mercedes-Benz was "engineered like no other car in the world."

Campaigns that build brands and businesses are founded on *big* ideas, marketing ideas that grow out of the product or service, ideas that are advertised with consistency and integrated into all sales communications. They do more than build brand images that have enduring value; truly big ideas move people to *action*.

WHAT MAKES A CAMPAIGN

A campaignable idea points the way clearly to fresh but related future advertisements. The essential ingredient of a campaign is a consistent look or feel.

Most campaigns embrace several elements of continuity and familiarity:

1. Visual similarity. A spokesperson is one way of providing a continuing visual image. The spokesperson can be a relevant personality like Karl Malden, wielding his tough-cop TV image for American Express Travelers Cheques. It can be a created character like Titus Moody, the Yankee deliveryman in his horse-drawn wagon, attesting to the old-fashioned goodness of Pepperidge Farm baked goods. It can even be an animal like Morris the Cat, for 9-Lives cat food.

Animal symbols are familiar visual campaign links—Budweiser's Clydesdale horses, the Dreyfus Fund lion stalking Wall Street. The Exxon tiger was introduced by the company (then Esso) in 1964, with the line "Rely on the tiger," later evolving into "Put a tiger in your tank." In 1972, the tiger helped bridge the change from Esso to Exxon with "We've changed our name but not our stripes."

Another kind of visual that holds a campaign together is a demonstration that appears in every advertisement, from a short sequence like the moisturizing cream that always pours into Dove beauty bar to the toys that run longer on Duracell batteries.

Insurance companies have discovered the metaphor as a campaign visual—Nationwide's blanket, Allstate's "good hands," Prudential's Rock of Gibraltar.

2. Verbal similarity. A catchy phrase isn't enough to make a campaign. Many purported campaign tag lines are just that—words at the end of the commercial that are too often throwaways and could be connected to any brand. Many others only have life and meaning after an extensive investment over time. By themselves on a piece of paper, they may not leap out as great and enduring.

The proper objective is a set of words that illuminates the advertising, encapsulates the promise, and can be associated with one brand only.

> *"Bermuda Shorts" for the Bermuda Office of Tourism identifies the brand name with its familiar symbol. Advertising in magazines and radio provides* short *descriptions of reasons to visit.*

Some other examples of strong campaign themes:

"Schweppervescence." (Schweppes.)

"For all you do, this Bud's for you." (Budweiser.)

"The temperature never drops below Zerex."

"M&M's melt in your mouth, not in your hand."

"The ultimate driving machine." (BMW.)

"Visine gets the red out."

"Have you driven a Ford lately?"

"Fly the friendly skies of United."

"The Heartbeat of America." (Chevrolet.)

"Good to the last drop." (Maxwell House coffee.)

A distinctive sound can help make a campaign promise sink in, like Campbell Soup's "Mmm-mmm, good," a 30-year-old promise that was revived after a hiatus, and Diet Pepsi's "You got the right one, baby—uh-huh." A distinctive voice or piece of music can also be an audible campaign signal.

3. Similarity of attitude. Some great campaigns don't even have a traditional theme line—or didn't have one when the campaigns were launched; what all the great campaigns do have is a consistent attitude toward the product and the people who use it.

> *There are few headlines and no copy or tag lines in Ralph Lauren advertising. Other than the name and the Polo symbol, each advertisement is different. Yet, whatever the product—clothing, home furnishings, fragrance—the campaign feel is one of quality, authenticity, classic styles, a nostalgic throwback to old values and old money.*

Attitude is an expression of brand personality; it is not a discretionary element used only in certain types of campaigns.

MARKETING IDEAS, NOT JUST ADVERTISING IDEAS

The most powerful and long-lasting campaigns derive from ideas that are built into the product and are then reflected in the advertising. Here are several examples of how a campaign grows organically out of a product or service.

American Airlines concluded that its superior on-time arrival performance could be another way to say quality—and a strong competitive theme. It persuaded the Department of Transportation to publish the on-time statistics of each airline; "The On-Time Machine" campaign was inextricably linked to the company's drive to excel on this point, and helped increase market share.

In its battle with AT&T, MCI came up with several highly advertisable services—a Friends and Family plan to attract subscribers with 20-percent discounts, and a personal 800 number that could be given as a gift to a frugal faraway grandmother.

"If you're like most women in America, you have three or four pairs of jeans in your wardrobe," starts a commercial for Lee Jeans. "One that's too small. One that's too big. One that's hopelessly out of fashion. And one that fits you every time you put them on." Lee Jeans makes several different lines that fit.

When most gasolines were being sold on low price, Shell added value with an ingredient that controlled deposits causing engine knock. SU 2000 super unleaded gasoline was introduced with a new pump to signal the change. The campaign increased Shell's market share and led to other added value automotive products for Shell.

It's not always necessary to improve products to come up with marketing ideas; often they are present in the product and need only to be cast in a new light by advertising.

Evolving a campaign The essence of American Express is extraordinary personal service around the world, embodied in one of the best-known promises in advertising, "Don't leave home without us." Under that banner, there are multiple products, services and campaigns, all supporting and lending credence to that central idea.

The two strategic elements that underlie American Express advertising are *prestige* and *service*. The prestige image was most visibly established with the "Do you know me?" campaign that promoted the American Express Card for 11 years. People famous in their own worlds but not necessarily known when visiting hotels or restaurants opened each commercial by asking, "Do you know me?" They attested that the American Express Card gained recognition even for famous people like them.

The prestige theme later shifted to print with a campaign in magazines. Striking photographs by Annie Leibovitz showed men and women of achievement, from musicians like Yo-Yo Ma and Ray Charles to athletes like Willie Shoemaker and Wilt Chamberlain.

But American Express is more than prestige; it is ultimately service to its Cardmembers around the world.

Cardmembers, not "card holders." The Card had long carried the line "Member since . . . " and the company had launched unique services like 24-hour card replacement, no preset spending limit, and other special benefits. "Member since . . . " led to the theme of the advertising—"Membership has its privileges."

There are other Card products (Gold Card, Optima, Corporate) and other campaigns (for restaurants, retail stores, hotels and other service establishments). There are promotions like cause-related marketing, which tie the use of American Express products to good causes in communities. There are targeted programs to extend the franchise to include more women professionals or students. There are other media, from small brochures in "Take One" displays to dioramas greeting travelers in airports around the world. And there are other products like Travel and Travelers Cheques.

With all of these products, markets, promotions, and campaigns, there are common elements that bind everything together:

■ a consistent personality and user image—*prestige*

■ a marketing idea—extraordinary personal *service* around the world

■ an umbrella advertising theme for the entire brand— "Don't leave home without us."

WHEN TO CHANGE CAMPAIGNS

Campaigns, even the most successful ones, do need to be refreshed. People change, products change, markets change. One way to lose a campaign is to preserve it reverently. Like products, campaigns must evolve, to stay relevant.

Freshen a campaign with new ideas and improved products.

There are times when campaigns wear out, in the sense that the market has changed so much that a new message is needed.

In England, Guinness Stout, a dark traditional brew, had been losing share for decades to lighter lager beers. That decline was reversed with a new campaign directly aimed at a new, younger audience. The advertising positioned the Guinness drinker as an individual who stands out from the crowd. The idiosyncratic campaign created a cult language among a younger audience, and sales followed.

Too often, advertisers change campaigns when deeper issues are causing the problem: pricing, outworn product, lack of distribution. Changing the campaign makes the situation worse by giving away the campaign equity as well as delaying dealing with the real issues.

Too often campaigns get discarded before they reach top potential. One research study indicates that the average TV campaign lasts only 17 months; the same study shows many campaigns are still building awareness and sales after three or four years.

A lot of time, energy, and money frequently go into developing backup campaigns, few of which ever run. It would be far more productive if the same amount of thought were invested in strengthening a current campaign that is working.

ORCHESTRATING A CAMPAIGN

There is a growing need to use a broad range of communications vehicles—direct marketing, sales promotion, and public relations, as well as media advertising—to reach fragmenting audiences. These services must be integrated to deliver a unified brand image and a single message to consumers, no matter which medium reaches them. A broad strategic overview is needed, with defined roles for each medium.

Whoever does the orchestrating must have a working knowledge of all major communications media and the mandate to get them to work together in a single campaign. You also need a big idea to orchestrate.

8 Media Strategies and Tactics

WHERE SHOULD YOU place your message? How often should it run and for how long?

Both these questions relate to yet another: How much should you spend?

They are the issues of media strategy.

With the growing segmentation of audiences and the proliferation of media options, a high degree of professionalism is required.

Put your money where your business is—or where you want it to be. "Fish where the fish are."

Media planning starts with a statement of objectives:

Who Do You Want to Reach? Describe your audience's demographics: their age, sex, income, education, family status—and buying habits.

Be precise. Not "Primary emphasis on men," but "70 percent of messages directed to men, 30 percent to women."

Describe their life-style or attitudes (*psychographics*).

Translate descriptions into actionable terms. Not "influentials," but "chief executive officers" or "directors of cultural institutions."

Describe how the decision process works.

Families are the best customers for fast-food restaurants. Parents make the decision to eat out and determine a bank of acceptable restaurants for the occasion; the child usually selects which one from that group.

When Do You Want to Reach Them? Do people buy your product year round, or primarily in the summer or on weekends or just when it rains? Some products are keyed to holidays: candy around Halloween, barbecue sauce for July 4th.

Be specific. What percent of messages should be allocated by quarter, by month, or even by the day of the week?

Allocate your media to periods when people decide to buy, not necessarily when they make the purchase.

The higher the price tag, the longer the lead time. Travel to Europe peaks in summer; the decision is made in spring.

Where Do They Live? All business is local and varies across the country. National marketers face a tough decision in geography—whether to advertise nationally or locally.

Be specific when describing key markets and what percent of business they represent. Total sales may be better in New York, but Bostonians may be better customers.

How Do You Want to Reach Them? What is the best environment for the prospect—and the advertising?

What other points should the media planner consider?

Some products have different growth curves than others. Typically, new packaged-goods products aim for high trial during the initial months, then try to sustain this level. Some products operate differently. People don't buy cold medicines until they have a cold. Awareness builds rapidly, but sales growth is slower. The same is true of dog foods; dog owners tend not to switch brands until the dog stops eating what's in the bowl.

MEDIA CONCEPTS

To read a media plan, you must understand media language. There are concepts basic to all media, plus some which apply only to broadcast or print (all are defined in the Glossary). Before jumping into some of the more technical concepts relating to media audiences, recognize a fundamental truth:

Advertising messages carried by the media are not necessarily absorbed by their audiences.

Viewers may leave the room or may just not notice a TV commercial. Magazine readers don't necessarily read or even see every ad. So in reality, the measured media audience is not the true measure of reaching the prospect. It is merely the *opportunity* to communicate.

Basic Concepts

Cost Per Thousand (CPM) is the cost of reaching 1,000 things, whether households or women or left-handed golfers. CPM is used to compare the relative efficiency of specific media.

If a television spot costs $100,000 and reaches 20 million homes, the CPM is $5.00 ($100,000 divided by 20,000, or one thousandth of 20 million).

Always ask, "Cost per thousand what?"

Reach is the number of different things (as with CPM) who have the opportunity to be exposed to a message at least once. It is also known as unduplicated or net audience or "cume."

A plan that gets to four out of five homes has a reach of 80.

Frequency is the number of times the message is potentially seen or heard in a defined period of time. It is usually expressed as an average. Reach and frequency are measured together over the same time period, commonly four weeks.

Frequency Distribution deals with the exact number of times individuals are exposed to advertising in a schedule.

Heavy viewers might be reached with a frequency of 12, light viewers with only one or two exposures.

Impressions represent the total number of messages delivered by a media plan, whatever the medium used: the number of people who see at least one message multiplied by the number of times they see it.

"Share of voice" is a brand's percent of impressions in a category compared to its competitors'.

Broadcast Concepts

Rating is the percent of homes or individuals tuned to the program. It's often reported on an average quarter-hour basis.

If two out of five homes are tuned to a program, it has a 40 rating.

Gross Rating Points (GRP) is the total of all rating points achieved for a specific schedule or campaign.

A plan with three 40-rated spots delivers 120 GRPs.

Plans calling for selectivity contain terms like WGRPs, for "women GRPs."

How to Use Reach and Frequency First, recognize that reach and frequency are interrelated. At a given rating level, as reach goes up, frequency goes down. You can't have both unless you add more rating points.

The relationship between reach, frequency, and rating points is expressed in this formula: $R \times F = GRP$. A plan that delivers a 90 reach and a frequency of four produces 360 GRPs in a four-week period (or 90 per week).

The ultimate issue: can the media plan achieve the goals of the strategy?

If your advertising objective is to get 50 percent of homes to be aware of your product or to try it, it cannot be done if the reach is less than 50 percent.

TWO KEYS TO SUCCESS

Most of the great success stories in advertising are ones of frequency and continuous advertising. They don't necessarily require big budgets.

David Ogilvy made Hathaway shirts into a leading brand with a tiny budget. At the beginning, all of the budget for "The Man in the Hathaway Shirt" was placed in one magazine, The New Yorker, *achieving frequency and continuity against a targeted audience.*

People's memories are short. College psychology courses confirm this finding, first reported by a German psychologist, Hermann Ebbinghaus, in 1885. Professor Ebbinghaus learned that

■ people forget 60 percent of what they learn within a half day.

■ the more repetition, the better retention.

■ forgetting is rapid immediately after learning, then levels off.

People Forget Quickly Advertisers who seek to reach a broad audience at the expense of sufficient frequency among key prospects risk wasting much of their investment.

For a product that is purchased frequently (soap or toothpaste, for example), the need for "reminder" advertising is obvious. It is also important to register the message for products purchased occasionally.

A case can be made for impact—concentrating everything into a dramatic program that rises above the clutter and

NIKE SHOES

Campaigns for each athletic line have distinctive personalities.

NYNEX YELLOW PAGES

Relevant humor draws attention to the product.

PEPPERIDGE FARM

Photography is usually more effective than artwork.

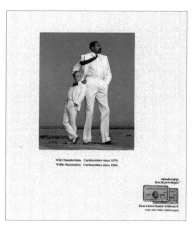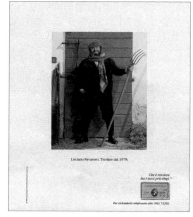

AMERICAN EXPRESS

"Portraits" of impressive Cardmembers work around the world.

ABSOLUT VODKA

A distinctive package shape is the visual campaign link.

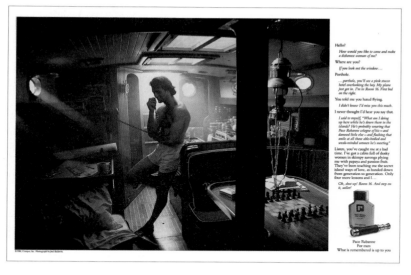

PACO RABANNE COLOGNE

An evocative setting creates story appeal that attracts readers.

BERMUDA TOURISM

Short messages reinforce the campaign concept and image.

Bill Heater
Age...30
Married, two children
Income...$35,000

Needs
Long-term security for
his family
To build investments

John Ventura, 43
Maggie Hines, 35
Brother and Sister

Needs
Start a joint investment pl
providing financial suppo
for parents.

You got to be making at least
twenty five? Yes?

Thirty?

Are you making thirty? Tell me.

Thirty, right?

Well...what've you got besides the car?

Investments? An IRA? Insurance?

No?

When are you going to do something?

You're not eighteen anymore.

Michael Mark
Age: 26
Single

Occupation Sales

| Income | $30,000 |

Assets	
Auto	$7,200
Cash	3,000

Estimated Expenses	
Income Tax	$8,000
Rent	5,400
Auto Loan and Insurance	3,000
Food, Clothing	4,100
Entertainment	3,600
Miscellaneous	2,400
	$26,500

Needs
Establish Financial Goals
Build Investments

Answers
John Hancock Personal Financial Analysis
John Hancock IRA
John Hancock Money Market Account

Michael Mark had a long talk with his older brother
last night. He reached the conclusion that things
weren't as great as they could be.

Later on, he had a conversation with a John Hancock
representative. These are the types of products
we recommended given his situation in life.

Think about where you are right now. Perhaps you'll
give us the opportunity to help you make the most out
of your real life situation.

Contact your nearest John Hancock representative for
more information or a current prospectus.

Real life, real answers.

JOHN HANCOCK FINANCIAL SERVICES
Involvement is key in the "Real life, real answers" campaign.

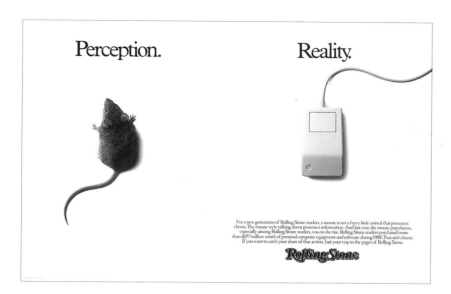

ROLLING STONE

Every advertisement is a complete sale. The visuals change; the headline never does.

HUGGIES

The benefit of diapers that don't sag or leak makes "Rockin' Rodger" a happy baby.

BUDWEISER

The campaign theme creates a strong user image among beer drinkers.

commands attention, rather than spreading it throughout the year. It's a seductive concept that relies on the *hope* that people will remember.

Repetition Aids Retention Advertising must be delivered with sufficient frequency to be effective, leading to another concept—*minimum effective reach.*

It is better to reduce the reach objective and concentrate on a smaller audience than to aim for a broad target with a small budget. That may mean advertising in fewer markets, advertising some products but not others, or advertising only in media that reach a precisely defined group of people.

Ideally, it would be great to advertise for 52 weeks. Since that isn't practical for most advertisers, compromises must be made between effective levels and budgets. One technique for doing this is *flighting*, the concentration of advertising into bursts, with a *hiatus* (no advertising) in between. It is better to begin at meaningful levels for brief periods—"flights" of four or six weeks each, for example—than to go to lower weekly levels for longer periods of time. Flighting can also be used to support promotions or to concentrate funds in key buying seasons.

The best of both worlds may be *pulsing*, continuous advertising plus periodic high-intensity bursts, to recognize seasonality, promotions, or other marketing considerations. Brands have different demands that influence the need for frequency, including purchase cycle, stage of development, competition, or the creative work itself. *The Wall Street Journal* underlines the importance of repetition in any effective campaign:

"Study after study has proven conclusively that the more people are exposed to your advertising, the more they will like your product and buy your product. Furthermore, the value of repetition is cumulative, which means that far too often advertising is pulled or replaced just as it's beginning to work."

The *Journal* cites studies by the Advertising Research Foundation and the Association of Business Publishers, by Alfred Politz Media Studies and by W. R. Simmons & Associates Research, and concludes:

"It's clear that creating a strong message is only a start. The more you repeat it, the stronger it gets."

The issue is not reach versus frequency, but reach *with* frequency.

HOW TO GET BETTER MEDIA PLANS

1. Agree in advance on media objectives and strategies. Make sure you understand the implications of the need for impact or continuity, minimum reach or frequency goals, the values assigned to different magazines, and so on. Goals must be consistent with and derived from the overall marketing plan. Media objectives are in reality one of the strategies to achieve marketing and advertising objectives.

2. Integrate the creative work into planning. Creative and media plans each start from the same strategic premise but then are executed on separate tracks. It is crucial that there is a working relationship between the two disciplines to assure the best environment for the message.

Should there be different campaigns for different media if a campaign doesn't work well in the recommended media? Not if the audience is the same. A good campaign has a memorable idea that should be able to translate to most media.

3. Look beyond the obvious. Do you need the visual impact of TV, or can you use a more selective medium? Do you need full pages in print? Why not direct mail? Think about your audience.

Disney PreSchool software needed to reach a hard-to-find audience—parents of two-to-six-year-old children in families with an IBM-compatible computer. They added direct mail to the media plan, inviting parents to a local mall to see a demonstration of the software. Seeing—and hearing—dramatically boosted software sales.

4. Look beyond cost per thousand. CPM is the weakest evaluation tool. It is a starting point, but it measures only cost, not effectiveness.

5. Think about clutter. Short message lengths look good in a media plan. They stretch media dollars by building frequency with fewer dollars. The facts support this: the average :15 spot is two thirds as effective as a :30—at only *half* the cost.

The problem is that more :15s reduce the effectiveness of all advertising through clutter, and a :15 can do a lot of things for a brand, but not everything. Use with restraint.

6. Recognize that all media plans are a compromise. The goal is to achieve a balance among options—reach, frequency, weeks of advertising, geography—and budget. Don't expect simple answers.

7. Balance local and national needs. Network television delivers unevenly across the country and may be under-delivering in some of your key markets. The plan will have to compensate with spot television, particularly in major markets. The same holds true for print. Magazines deliver differently from area to area.

8. Evaluate alternative plans. The best way to determine how well the plan meets the objectives is to look at several tactical alternatives. Since the media plan is highly quanti-fiable, it is easy to check the plan in terms of the specific goals set for it.

9. Tie the plan closely to marketing goals. If the brand's objective is to maintain market position, allocate spending where the brand's sales are high expressed as a percentage of population—a *brand development index* (BDI). To expand and grow in new markets, consider an allocation based on where the brand is weak but other brands sell well—a *category development index* (CDI).

10. Be creative. Media plans can be creative too.

- *Hallmark introduced its new line of Shoe Box greeting cards with samples tipped in magazines.*

- *Seagram's broke through the weekend sports telecast clutter by developing a minishow for its wine coolers: "Seagram's Game Summary."*

- Sports Illustrated *reached advertising agency media buyers with posters in mid-Manhattan bus stop shelters near the offices of advertising agencies.*

Creativity is not limited to the creative department.

HOW MUCH TO SPEND ON ADVERTISING

This is as much a business decision as a media question, but media planning can provide part of the answer. You must be prepared to *invest* whatever is required to do the job. Better to stay home and not advertise at all than to invest too little.

There are computer models that theorize a relationship between profitability, market share, and media spending, but they require evaluation in the marketplace. There are business analysis techniques a media planner can use to gauge how much to spend, which include several factors:

■ How much is competition spending?

■ What is their market share—and share of voice?

■ What is your market-share goal?

■ How much must you invest to have a share of voice equal to your share of market?

■ What are your basic requirements for coverage, frequency, and weeks of advertising?

■ Are there standards for advertising-to-sales ratios or cost per unit of sales?

For a new product, the spending level is part of a test market plan.

Alternative spending levels can be tested. Test in at least two other markets, and test only levels that vary by 50 percent; anything smaller is too small to read.

For an established, successful product, continually test how far is up. Try higher spending levels, new media, new markets.

MEDIA DEVELOPMENT

The media world is reinventing itself so rapidly that it is important to keep a sensible perspective. Don't get carried away with the new technologies, the new opportunities—and predictions about the demise of some media.

The decline of the mass media—network television and mass-market magazines—and the rise of targeted media—cable TV and specialized magazines—are facts. Network shares have eroded to close to 60 percent of households, and some famous national magazines have gone under. But mass media will not disappear. If there were no national network television, someone would have to invent it. And there will always be a place for broad-interest national publications. There are, however, dramatic changes taking place in the media world.

Broadcast "Advances in video technology are likely to transform television," reports *The New York Times*. Fiber-optic cable and digital video compression can expand the number of cable channels available to 300. Many will be pay-per-view, available at the touch of a button.

With cable reaching 60 percent of homes, the opportunities for targeted programming and niche marketing increase considerably. There will be more foreign language stations, community news, telemarketing channels (some people call them "flea TV"), the same movie starting at different times on different channels.

Interactive TV will also change the way many people watch television. Viewers will be able to alter the programming to suit their interests, choosing the content of a program (the level of difficulty in an exercise class, which Olympic event to watch) or even the camera angle in a sports event. With this degree of precision, advertising too can be even more precise, selling the appropriate model of a car to the appropriate audience.

It will soon be possible to have "pure video" on demand—to access an encyclopedia, for example, or call up old movies from a film library.

Another influence on television is the VCR. VCRs are in seven out of ten homes, yet A. C. Nielsen reports that owners continue to watch TV much as they always have. While there is some erosion in viewing the commercial, Ogilvy & Mather points out that the impact is surprisingly moderate and two out of three commercials are left intact. The fear of "zapping," at least today, seems to be overstated.

Print Publications are making it possible for advertisers to run print spectaculars: advertisements that talk, pop up, or come with 3-D glasses. According to a Starch research report, pop-ups produce significantly higher readership scores. More important, magazines are harnessing the power of subscriber data bases.

Time, Inc., has a computer-controlled process that allows advertisers in Time, People, Sports Illustrated, *and* Money *to address specific market segments with custom-tailored advertising messages. Advertisers can pinpoint three groups: recent movers, high-income seniors, and direct responders.*

With selective binding, L. L. Bean delivered one message to Time *subscribers who were already on their mailing list. Other subscribers were invited to send for a catalog.*

With sophisticated laser printing, magazines can personalize advertisements for each subscriber by name—in effect, direct mail in a magazine.

There is agreement that special-interest magazines will continue to proliferate, and that their focus will narrow considerably. Beyond titles like *Car and Driver*, there may be ones like *Nissan Novice* or *Mercedes Mechanic*.

Nontraditional Media Other media that reach very specific audiences include everything from shopping carts in supermarkets to airline in-flight videos, from messages on ski lifts to maps that carry restaurant advertisements.

While they provide an attractive opportunity to meet clear objectives, these nontraditional media don't do the job on their own. It's best to use them selectively, since they are neither measurable nor accountable.

Maybelline returned to mainstream television after investing heavily in nontraditional sponsorship projects, citing a fuzzy image and lack of consumer presence as the reasons.

A good plan relies on creativity to get the most out of proven media principles.

9 Promotions That Add Value

"WHAT'S THE HOT promotion of the '80s?" asked the headline in *Advertising Age*. The answer: cash refunds. What was the hot promotion of the '70s according to the same report? Cents-off coupons.

For two decades, the ultimate promotion was to cut the price of products. A coupon may be a good idea, but it's not a promotion. Promotion consultant Steve Arbeit calls refunds and coupons "demotions," because they lower the value of the brand in the mind of the consumer.

THE SHIFT IN POWER TO THE RETAILER

Sales promotion is a huge business, almost twice as large as advertising and growing faster. However, two thirds of reported promotion spending is in trade deals, including display allowances, slotting allowances, case allowances, and other price-cutting promotions.

One of the reasons for the shift of marketing funds

from advertising to promotion is the change in the speed of information flow. When a campaign was judged in part by quarterly Nielsen reports, advertising had time to work. When scanner data says what ran on Thursday had no results on Friday, coupons, contests, or sweepstakes are a quick fix—but the risk is that brands become commodities, with price the only difference between them.

If you can only sell a product with a coupon, a rebate, or another way to disguise a price cut, then the consumer is telling you that the product is not worth the asking price.

The role of promotion is to stimulate short-term sales. Good promotion—*strategic promotion*—also reinforces the image of the brand and adds to its value.

BUILDING VALUE WITH PROMOTION

Here are some value-building promotion principles:

1. Make it relevant. Too many promotions are created in a vacuum—"Let's run a sweepstakes," or "Let's sponsor a golf tournament." Start with a strategy and look for promotions that grow organically from a unified marketing plan.

In London, the Financial Times *celebrated its 100th anniversary with a promotion aimed at turning occasional readers into regular ones. It mounted a contest that required collecting numbered tokens from six consecutive issues.*

Prizes were related to the interests of the readers, and presented in understated FT style:

- *100 gallons of petrol—and an Audi.*

- *100 magnums of Laurent Perrier Champagne—to be collected from Laurent Perrier in France.*

- *100 rolls of photo film—and a Kenya safari to shoot them on.*

- *100 records—and a round-the-world trip with evenings at famous opera houses.*

During the 12-week promotion, circulation of the FT increased steadily, compared to a decline for the same period the previous year.

The best promotions reinforce the brand personality. Nynex extended its multimedia "If it's out there, it's in here" campaign for the yellow pages with a relevant promotion—sweepstakes. Consumers were asked to look up the "heading of the day" in the telephone book and note the page. Then, 1,000 telephone calls were made at random. Winners received $1,000 to spend with the Nynex category of their choice.

2. Pretest promotions. Pretesting need not be expensive. For packaged goods, you can use small samples of typical households, or just a few stores for readable in-store tests. Split-store panels can be quickly checked with UPC scanning systems.

If you offer a coupon, test the face value and the way it is delivered: by mail, in a newspaper or magazine, or on-pack.

Research shows that redemption rates for a coupon offer can vary from two to 25 percent, depending on the coupon value, the creative approach, and the method of delivery.

If you offer a premium, make sure of its appeal.

For services and non–packaged-goods products, where scanning data is not used, direct mail and on-site audits are used.

3. Track the results. Keep records of promotions and how they've worked. Look for trends and patterns, and establish principles that guide future programs.

Capture knowledge over time.

4. Keep it simple. If the idea is easy to grasp quickly, it's more likely to succeed.

> *To increase sales of its dental care section, Safeway stores in England ran a promotion with special appeal to children: "Free 50p from the Tooth Fairy." Children had to complete a chart confirming they had brushed their teeth twice daily for four weeks; this was signed by a parent or guardian and sent with two proofs of purchase from any dental care product. The Safeway Tooth Fairy sent back 50 pence and a certificate.*

If a promotion comes with three pages of rules, turn it down.

5. Advertise trial-builders. If you're running a promotion designed to build loyalty among current users, such as a coupon in the package, advertising directed at a broad audience is frequently wasted. But a promotion aimed at encouraging trial among new users is usually worth supporting with advertising. The general rule of thumb is: add advertising only when you need to achieve a measurable increment over what the promotion could achieve on its own.

6. Don't count on promotion alone. Nielsen has done hundreds of studies that show price promotions work best with new brands or with established brands with a major product improvement. Conversely, an established brand with a strong franchise of loyal users is less affected by competitive coupon campaigns.

A Harvard Business School study showed three brands in a price promotion war increased total sales only three percent while profits were cut by 36 percent. Further, it showed the brand that also advertised was hurt the least.

The moral of this story: don't rent consumers. Short-term incentives do not take the place of a compelling long-term reason to buy. There will always be someone who is prepared to sell for less.

7. Build campaigns. A key contribution of promotion is that it brings the advertising to life via special events, lifestyle programs, sampling in malls, etc.

The fun personality of Kool-Aid is extended by Wacky Warehouse. Kids collect Kool-Aid points (offered on the package) and mail in for merchandise—Kool-Aid Man mugs, wristwatches, and other items that add dimensions to the brand.

Orchestrated promotional events contribute to brand image.

To stimulate the sale of Maxwell House brands and of coffee drinking in general, several brands were combined in an umbrella promotion campaign, "Coffee Breaks." The campaign offered at various times a coffee thermos, coffee mugs, coffee recipes, holiday canisters.

A promotion strategy includes objectives, a profile of the target audience, the unique role that promotion will play, and how the program will be evaluated.

8. Involve the trade. What's the hot promotion of the '90s? Customized promotions tailored to the trade and the consumer.

Carrier involved its air conditioner dealers by sponsoring the Junior Olympics and shared the sponsorship in each town with the local dealer.

9. Look for big ideas. "You can't find big ideas unless you're looking for them, unless you need them, unless you insist upon them," says Jerry Welsh, the marketing whiz who created cause-related marketing—among other big ideas—for American Express. "You've got to believe that big ideas are not merely nice to have but are the heart of our success."

The cause-related marketing program at American Express started with local promotions supporting a community resource like a zoo. For every use of the American Express Card and each new card or purchases of Travelers Cheques, American Express agreed to contribute a certain amount to the local cause.

It worked in local communities across the U.S., building distribution as well as consumer sales; it worked as a national promotion, supporting the restoration of the Statue of Liberty. It worked around the world. An example of doing well by doing good.

10. Build relationships. What's the next big idea? Most probably, relationship marketing, with promotions customized to individual consumer life-styles and delivered personally by direct mail.

A DISPLAY ONLY WORKS IF IT IS DISPLAYED

Without advertising, quipped comedian Lily Tomlin, people would wander aimlessly up and down supermarket aisles. Underlying that lighthearted line is an element of truth, as one discovers by visiting a store in another country with another culture. Even well-known brands in familiar surroundings benefit from in-store promotion that points the way.

There are in effect two targets for effective in-store material.

■ *It must be something that the <u>retailer</u> wants to display.*

■ *It must be a compelling story to the <u>consumer</u>.*

This is a reversal of the historic priority of designing displays (and promotions) primarily for consumers. It recognizes the shift in power from manufacturer to retailer.

Store managers like appealing POP (point-of-purchase) displays. They help move merchandise and make stores more exciting. They must also conform to the store image and its display policies.

A good display can increase the level of trade support, move the brand on its merits (without price-cutting), sell anywhere in the store (checkouts, for example), organize and accommodate your entire line, and provide strong brand identification. The proliferation of scanners is producing hard evidence about sales and the effect of displays.

A study by Information Resources, Inc., covering 2,400 grocery stores, showed that on average, displays yield almost eight times the incremental sales of a 15-percent (unadvertised) discount. This means a single week of display for a single product will gain the same amount of sales volume as two months of price discounting alone.

Some display principles to think about:

■ **Involve the trade.** Include something the retailer needs or wants—a price board, a clock, or some premium to take home.

■ **Involve your customer.** When you can involve consumers at the point of purchase, you bring them closer to the sale. Encourage consumers to pick up a product, to try it or feel it.

> *Teledyne's Water Pik shower massage enables the consumer to feel the pulsating action—without getting wet. The display, created by Thomson Leeds, uses a specially designed membrane. Sales increase over 300 percent when the unit is used.*

■ **Pull people into the store.** Promotions based around events like the Olympics are proven traffic builders. So are displays that are custom-designed with retailers, who know what interests their customers.

> *Some promotions ask the consumer to check a number on a direct-response mailing against the winning number on display in the store.*

■ **Let your package do the selling.** Improved printing techniques allow products to be merchandised even on the cardboard shipping container—the "inside-outside shipper."

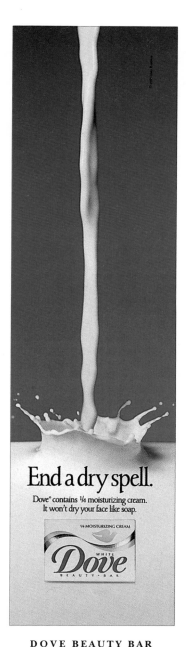

End a dry spell.

Dove® contains ¼ moisturizing cream.
It won't dry your face like soap.

¼ MOISTURIZING CREAM

Dove
WHITE
BEAUTY · BAR

WHAT LITTLE TRAFFIC there is in
Lynchburg, Tennessee can be brought to a
standstill by a Mallard hen.

This one came from over by our limestone cave
spring, where Jack Daniel discovered water so
right for whiskey making (it's iron-
free), he built his distillery alongside.
Of course, that meant sharing the
property with a few ducks. But to
have a source of water this treasured,
we've always been glad to stop
for friends who value it as much
as we do.

SMOOTH SIPPIN'
TENNESSEE WHISKEY

MRS. MARY BOBO is the most special
person in Lynchburg, Tennessee. This July,
she's more special than ever.

Mrs. Bobo has run the boarding house in town
since 1908. And though she's never served a
drop of whiskey in it, she's been a friend of our
distillery every one of those
years. This year, Miss Mary
will be 99 years old. Everyone at the distillery will be
sending her a card. If you're
a friend of Jack Daniel's,
we hope you might like
to send her one too.

CHARCOAL
MELLOWED
♢
DROP
♢
BY DROP

DOVE BEAUTY BAR
*"One-quarter moisturizing cream" is the
reason-why for softer skin.*

JACK DANIEL'S
*Understatement is a good strategy
for premium products.*

AMERICAN FLORAL MARKETING COUNCIL
Look for human, emotional content in outdoor advertising.

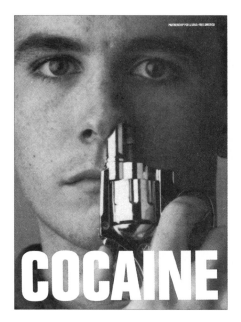

PARTNERSHIP FOR A DRUG-FREE AMERICA
A public service campaign from an agency coalition.

DIET PEPSI
*Relevant entertainment draws
viewers to the commercial.*

DURACELL
*Scenarios with battery-powered toys
demonstrate product superiority.*

Jeans for life's little ups and downs.

Lee jeans are designed to fit the natural curves of a woman's body. But most importantly, they're designed to fit the natural curves of a woman's life. Nobody fits your body....or the way you live...better than Lee.

E L A S T I C · R I D E R

Lee
The brand that fits.

LEE JEANS
Jeans that fit is a marketing idea built into the product.

BEWARE OF CHEAP IMITATIONS

There are a lot of insulations around. Including some that may come to you claiming to be "just as good as" the famous Pink® original. They may even tempt you with "bargain" prices.

But when you add up the extras you get by carrying the pink McCoy, you quickly see that the pretenders are being pretty miserly.

A great pink product, backed to the hilt by America's leading insulation company, is just the beginning.

You also get the important benefit of Owens-Corning's unmatched, multimillion-dollar advertising. Year after year, through two decades, Owens-Corning has outspent all competitors on national TV and in print to *pre-sell* your customers. Research shows they now arrive at your store preferring pink Fiberglas® insulation 5-to-1 over other brands.

The color pink is such a powerful selling tool, in fact, that Owens-Corning has been awarded a Federal *trademark* on it!

You get the advantage of Owens-Corning sales promotions, too—like truckload sales or offers of NFL football jackets. These promotions build store traffic for the entire range of merchandise you carry.

And, of course, Owens-Corning's hard-working point-of-sale aids—colorful displays, posters, brochures, and counter cards—are second to none.

Finally, the image of quality surrounding Owens-Corning's building products enhances your own reputation as a first-class outlet for top merchandise. Which, in turn, keeps your sales and profits in the pink.

FIBERGLAS

OWENS-CORNING FIBERGLAS
The Pink Panther brands pink fiber-glass insulation.

FORD

"Have you driven a Ford lately?" is a strong verbal campaign link.

COTTON INC.

An emotional promise underlines the rational benefits of the fabric.

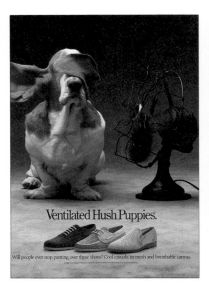

HUSH PUPPIES
*Layouts are clear and poster-like
in their simplicity.*

UNITED NEGRO COLLEGE FUND
*A public service campaign sponsored
by the Advertising Council.*

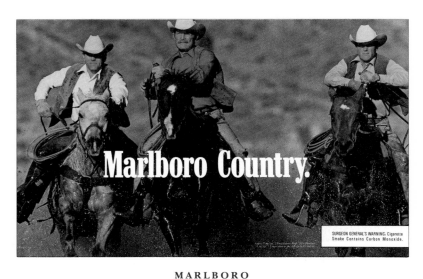

MARLBORO
A long-running campaign with consistent imagery.

A SPECTATOR'S GUIDE TO BRITISH POMP & CIRCUMSTANCE.

TWA Getaway Vacations. An affordable way to see Britain in Heritage '84.

No matter what time of year you visit Britain, you'll never miss the pageantry. Some events take place daily, some annually, but most haven't changed over the years and all are living links with the past. And in this, Britain's Heritage Year, you'll find more pageantry than ever.

The *Changing of the Guard* at Buckingham Palace takes place at 11:30 every morning beginning in April (every other morning until then), but be there by 11 to ensure a good view. The guards also stand duty at *St. James's Palace* and *Windsor Castle.*

On June 16, her a 41-gun salute fired in honor of the *Queen's Official Birthday.* And *Trooping the Colour*—a ceremony in which the Colour of one of the Foot Guards' Regiments is paraded before the Queen. Even en route to the ceremony, the guards are a spectacular sight to see.

Visit the *Royal Mews* and see all the Queen's coaches and horses, including the *Coronation Coach.*

There will be over fifty *Highland Gatherings* in Scotland. The largest is the *Royal Highland Gathering* at Braemar, Deeside, on September 1.

The *Edinburgh International Festival* featuring music and drama will be held from August 12 through September 1.

Don't miss the *Military Tattoo* which takes place from August 10 to September 1 on the floodlit esplanade of Edinburgh Castle.

There's no better way to experience the pomp

and circumstance of Britain than with TWA on a Getaway Vacation.

TWA Getaway Vacations. The best of Britain. For less.

Most of TWA's twelve Getaway Vacations to Britain are priced lower than last year. Take, for instance, TWA's *London Theatre and Countryside.* For just $429 to $548, you get ten days to explore the regal capital and the historic English countryside. You'll start with several days in London, where you'll get tickets to two top shows in the famous West End—the Broadway of Britain. There's a half-day guided tour that includes a visit to Westminster Abbey, Big Ben and Buckingham Palace. (You can always tell when the Queen is home—the Royal Standard is flown.) And you'll have enough free time to explore London on your own.

Then you're off to the countryside by private motorcoach. See Windsor Castle, the Royal Family's home on the River Thames. The university city of Oxford. Stratford-upon-Avon, Shakespeare's birthplace. And Stonehenge where the ancient monoliths stand.

Throughout, you'll stay in hotels with private bath or shower. Daily Continental breakfasts are included in London, full English breakfasts and dinners in the countryside.

Super Values with TWA's Super Saver Vacations.

TWA's Super Saver *"Britain,"* for example, is a fourteen-day tour of the splendors of England, Scotland and Wales—for

just $529 to $389. You'll see London's Westminster Abbey and Buckingham Palace. Visit Cambridge and York by private motorcoach. Then Edinburgh, Scotland. The Lake District. Wales, the land of castles. Historic Stonehenge and more. All along, your vacation includes hotels with private bath or shower, daily Continental breakfasts and dinners in many of the towns.

All TWA's low airfares are per person, double occupancy, not including airfare.

TWA's low airfares make it easy.

This year TWA's airfares are low and the dollar is high. And that really makes Great Britain a great bargain.

For more information, send for your Britain Heritage '84 and TWA Getaway Britain brochures. Then see your travel agent.

It's Britain's Heritage Year—a spectacular time to travel to a land where spectacle is a proud tradition.

BRITAIN

Send to: British Tourist Authority
Box 10501
Long Island City, NY 11101
or, Box 8000
Van Nuys, CA 91409
Please send me your free brochures.

Name _____
Address _____
City _____
State _____ Zip _____

TWA GETAWAY VACATIONS
EASILY THE TIME OF YOUR LIFE.

BRITISH TRAVEL AUTHORITY

Long, fact-packed copy works when people are investing time or money.

NUPRIN

The campaign theme registers the brand name with the promise.

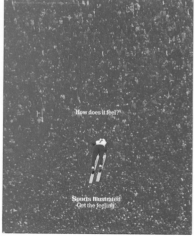

SPORTS ILLUSTRATED

Fans get the "get the feeling" of being there — in the magazine's pages.

POLO BY RALPH LAUREN

The campaign portrays a lifestyle and attitude with photographs alone.

■ **Tailor your display.** Neighborhoods and stores are different. So are various types of stores; for example, self-service versus full-serve.

■ **Tie in to your advertising.** Use key visuals to present a unified image.

■ **Make the display easy to set up.** And easy to take care of.

Tetley tea uses prepacked shipping cartons that unfold into a display, with no setup time.

■ **Remember seasons and holidays.** Good reasons for a store manager to *want* to put up your display.

■ **Emphasize clear, bold graphics.** The retail environment is visually cluttered. Use symbols, images, and messages that communicate.

■ **The product—not the display—is the hero.** If possible, locate the display apart from the usual product location. Try to make it compatible with another category—a wine display in the cheese section, a pretzel display in the beer aisle.

Promotions in stores can do something not possible in any other medium—they can let people experience the product. The opportunity to let consumers see, feel, smell, or taste products is well understood by retailers, less appreciated by advertisers. Many products come in antiseptic boxes or cans; in-store sampling or customized promotions with retailers enable the products to come out of their packages. Don't underestimate the power of sensory appeals to get people to try your product.

PRODUCT PUBLICITY

The art of product publicity is to get a third party—
the media—to talk about your product in a favorable
manner. Third-party endorsements by columnists, authors, editors, reporters, and TV news personalities carry
a clout that paid advertising cannot.

Get your story to life-style editors, broadcast-news assignment editors, talk show producers, and trade publications. Give them a "hook" that makes it newsy.

> *To support its introduction of Hero cologne, Chesebrough-
> Pond's sponsored the Big Brother program to show that
> everyday men can be heroes in their local communities.*

Sometimes it's necessary to build the appropriate promotion values into the product. Not many people were eating
"horse mackerel" salads or sandwiches until a persuasive
PR man renamed the product "tuna fish."

Harold Burson, a dean of the PR business, believes in
advertising *with* publicity. Says Burson:

> *"First, it enhances the credibility of the advertising message.
> The publicity must be timed to appear first; then when
> people see the ads, they pay attention.*

> *"It also extends the message. There is a tyranny in the 30-
> second commercial that a news story can overcome, by
> providing more information."*

THINK HEADLINES AND MESSAGES

What is the headline you would like to see for your product or service? What are the messages you want delivered?

The primary PR tools are news releases and press kits.
However, a news release is unlikely on its own to produce

the desired headlines or stories. There are several tactics that command attention: press conferences for news that won't wait; video releases or satellite feeds; media tours. The best way to get a good story is the less dramatic but effective one-on-one tailored presentation, with a journalist with whom someone has built a long-term relationship of candor and respect.

Publicity people must also have a nose for news. They must consider every story in the news for what it could mean to your product, then pitch that story to the media.

Sometimes a high-visibility advertising campaign is news in itself, like the Bo Jackson "Bo Knows" campaign for Nike. Nike carefully orchestrated the "Bo Show" spot for the Major League Baseball All-Star Game—an exclusive to the Associated Press. Then media kits and video, with "interview bites" from its star athletes, went to 100 print and TV reporters.

At the dramatic end of the spectrum are sponsorships and special events, tying promotion in with music tours, entertainment shows, or major sports events like the Olympics, marathons, tennis or golf tournaments, or auto races. These events have high visibility, are highly targeted, and extend naturally to the media and into wherever the product or service is sold. They become a focal point for integrating all marketing and communications efforts.

CREATING A COMMUNICATIONS PROGRAM

Start with the assumptions that a publicity program is accountable, and the way to measure its success is not with stacks of press clippings.

Set actionable objectives. Segment the publics—the media and *their* audiences—and get agreement on the messages for each audience. Then outline a plan of action for each audience. *Measure the results.* Concentrate on quality and results against the objectives. Talk to the sales force, add an 800 number to press releases, conduct prepost attitudinal surveys.

Brands cannot live by promotion alone. Nor can promotions work effectively without strong brands.

10 Brochures and Sales Pieces

PAMPHLETS ARE THE oldest advertising medium. They go back to the 12th century, to a love poem in a little booklet. They have promoted partisan views that kicked off revolutions. They may be small in size, but they loom large in business. Not everyone has a budget for media advertising, but almost every business needs and produces promotional materials.

Some brochures are clearly more effective than others, attracting more attention, inviting readers, and increasing sales. Others are a waste of time and production money.

Certain principles in the creation of brochures are similar to those for print ads. Many, however, are unique to sales pieces and can contribute greatly to the effectiveness of the message.

Start with strategy.

Advertising and sales pieces should march to the same drummer. The visuals, words, and personality of the brochure should remind readers of the advertisements.

Study the competition—and discover where you have an edge. Understand your target audience.

BETTER BROCHURES

1. Put your selling message on the cover. The cover of a brochure works like the headline of a print advertisement. State your position, or promise a benefit to the reader.

> *The Hotel Manypany in the French West Indies has an award-winning brochure with a clear positioning on the cover: "A tiny refuge from the world. For the very worldly."*

The cover should tell the reader who you are, where you are, and what you are.

2. Be single-minded. Most brochures fail because they try to show everything and tell everything, so they end up with dozens of postage-stamp-size photos and lengthy copy that speaks to many different audiences. Try this discipline. If you had to use only *one* photograph in the entire piece, which would it be? If the penguin is hands down the most popular attraction of your zoo, your selection is made.

3. Use a single illustration on the cover. Research says that one large illustration is more effective than several small ones. And illustrations with story appeal and bright colors involve the reader.

4. Always caption photographs. Captions are read almost twice as often as body copy, yet no more than one out of five brochures bothers to caption photos. Captions that give the reader lots of pithy information work harder than short bland ones.

"The Monterey Bay Aquarium is the newest, largest, spiffiest in the world. There's a kelp cathedral, a giant reef and a gang of baby otters that were raised on a waterbed." That's the enticing caption of a brochure for the state of California.

5. Avoid clichés. Visual clichés abound in brochures. The smiling chef appears in every hotel brochure; the smiling bikini-clad temptress in every travel piece. If you are likely to see a visual in your competition's brochure, *don't use it.*

6. Load it with facts. The most frequent criticism of brochures is that they "don't give enough facts." Tell consumers what is included, the price, the hours. Graphic devices such as bullets and grids can highlight information.

Consumers prefer practical, useful information, such as what the climate is like in your area and whether a tie is required in your hotel dining room.

7. Make your piece worth keeping. Give your piece a longer life. Brochures that unfold into posters suitable for framing are one example; yearly calendars of events are another.

8. Give your product a first-class ticket. Don't stint on quality. In many cases, the brochure *is* your product. If your budget is limited, consider doing a smaller mailer or an elegant black-and-white piece instead of using four colors. Use of one color plus black-and-white is another alternative.

9. Use the envelope to deliver a message. Tease the readers, whet their appetites, promise them a benefit for reading on.

A summer theater on Long Island mails brochures in May. The envelope promises, "Subscribe now. See four plays for as little as $35." The theater has tripled subscriptions.

10. Ask for the order. What action do you want the reader to take? Write, telephone, send a check—every brochure should contain a clear call to action.

Travel Brochures

The travel, tourism, and hospitality industries—including ski areas, theme parks and attractions—are the heaviest users of brochures. They share a number of challenges: diffuse target audiences (business travelers, pleasure seekers, travel professionals); a need to present lots of information in one brochure; schizophrenic brand personalities (one benefit in high season, a different one in off-season).

The most important principle is to identify an umbrella positioning and stick with it, for all audiences and all seasons.

Announcing news is helpful for travel and tourism; for amusements and attractions it is lifeblood. Visitors are drawn to return by a promise of new adventures. The best place to announce news is on the cover; you can make the old cover last one more year by using an overlay or snipe.

CATALOGS

There are thousands of catalogs in print, featuring everything from boomerangs and cookie cutters to men's and women's clothing. Shopping by mail has increased dramatically as people's leisure time has decreased. Another significant development is the consumer's willingness to buy more high-priced items through catalogs.

These principles for more effective catalogs apply whether you are selling nasturtium bulbs or fishing tackle.

■ **The cover is your showcase.** If you put a product on the cover, it will sell three times better than if it were placed on an inside page. The cover also sets the personality for the catalog.

> *Garden catalogs, almost without exception, show flowers on the cover—usually new introductions or special collections, never seeds. The Burpee Seed Company sells more vegetable seeds in their catalog than flower seeds. But flowers on the cover make the catalog work better.*

Other traditional "hot spots"—places in the catalog where merchandise tends to attract more notice—include the back cover, inside front and back covers, the center spread, the page next to the order form, and page one.

■ **Make it easy for customers to order.** Organize your layout so readers can pair descriptions with photos. A bound-in order blank helps; so does a postage-paid envelope. Allow the customer ample space to write in necessary information, such as the number of a credit card.

> *Catalogs have a long life. If you bind in an order form, always include complete order information separately within*

the catalog as well. Prospects will read it long after the form has been torn out.

■ **Don't waste space.** Make every inch of your catalog contribute to the sale. For some products, the most efficient use of space is a full-page photo; for others, many photos on a page work harder. L. L. Bean, which has been mailing its catalog for over 70 years, uses three or four smaller visuals on every page, with long descriptive copy.

■ **Pack the copy with facts, not fantasy.** The trick, say professional catalog writers, is to *anticipate* the consumer's questions and answer them in the copy. The more you tell, the more you sell, especially when the product is an expensive one or involves the customer's well-being.

"The people who are going backpacking, for instance, depend on our products for their comfort," says a spokesperson for Eddie Bauer, sellers of outdoor clothing and equipment. "They are vitally interested in details about buttons, zippers, wind resistance. These customers read every word."

■ **Location shooting adds excitement.** Photographic sessions outside a studio add a note of visual excitement and let you take advantage of natural light. Location shoots can be as simple as the park across the street or as complex as a trip around the world. Use of locations is more effective when it is relevant to the product.

Saks Fifth Avenue added romance to a collection of Scottish patterns by photographing the models in front of historic ruins and Highland scenery.

■ **Change pace now and then.** Horchow's pioneered the technique of devoting a full-page or even a two-page spread to unique items. The visual surprise calls attention to the merchandise and also serves as a refreshing change in layout.

Bloomingdale's added interest to its Christmas catalog, with the theme, "Be an angel, too." It featured nine celebrities sharing their holiday memories and invited everyone who read the catalog to make a charitable contribution too.

■ **Repeat your winners.** Always include those tried-and-true products that never fail to garner orders. Give new items a good position so you can evaluate how well they perform. Establish a level of performance, and weed out merchandise that fails to meet it.

■ **Mail to your list often.** Professionals say it pays to mail four, five, six times a year—and more. Mail even more often to your best customers; they are your best prospects.

Test-mail your catalog more than once in the same season. Give it a fresh look by changing the cover.

Consider producing a smaller, less expensive minicatalog to mail when you are prospecting for new customers.

The catalog must represent you at your best. Tell the truth, create a desire to purchase, and instill confidence.

BETTER PRODUCTION FOR LOWER COSTS

The key to better production and controlled costs is simply *planning*. Allow 120 days from the start of creative work to delivery of a finished product from the printer.

When production costs run over budget, overtime is

usually the culprit. Understand how much time each phase requires, and allow ample time for each: photography, retouching, typesetting, proofreading, engraving, and printing. For example, the rule of thumb for engraving is 10 days.

■ **Put a production schedule in writing.** Include time for corrections between every step. Don't assume everything will be right the first time.

■ **Order paper early.** The single biggest cost for most jobs is the printer's order of paper. Since paper costs seem to rise continually, the earlier the printer can order, the more you save. You'll also know that you can count on the type of paper you want.

■ **Ask for three print bids.** Unless you have an extraordinary working relationship with a printer, get bids from three. Be sure they all have the right equipment for your job. You are not bound to take the lowest bid, but the process helps to assure you of a fair price.

■ **Approve copy before setting type.** Read copy carefully for content and spelling while it is still in manuscript. The time for changes is at this stage, not after it has been set. Get legal approvals early.

If a number of people must approve copy, ask them to sign the manuscript as an indication of approval.

You can save 15 percent or more on typesetting charges by stern control of copy approval.

■ **Lots of small photographs mean higher production costs.** A page with several small photographs is more expensive than a page with one large one. Each color photograph must be individually color-separated.

A *tip on photography:*

For extra impact and a fresh, bold look, blow up small details for extra impact. Use a part to suggest the whole.

■ **Allow for special effects.** Features such as gatefolds and effects such as pop-ups or die cuts can add impact to the brochure. They also add to your costs, so budget for them early.

■ **Think about delivery costs.** The weight of the brochure is an important consideration. Do you want to be able to mail it first class? Will any other material be mailed with the brochure? If so, allow for that weight too. Check with the post office.

Over the centuries, brochures have wooed lovers, started wars and changed ideas. They are small but potent marketing tools you can use effectively either in addition to advertising or on their own.

11 Global Brands

COCA-COLA, SONY, LEVI'S, Mercedes-Benz, Pepsi, Benetton, Canon, Marlboro, American Express, Nestlé, Gillette, Martell, McDonald's—all are established global brands with a unified positioning.

More open markets, international travel and communications, and international advertising contribute to more global brands. Cultural phenomena such as popular music, rock music stars, and movies are making this easier; entertainment is a global language.

International media are also fueling this trend, including satelite television; CNN, the Cable News Network which is seen in 94 countries; and MTV, reaching 100 million households in 37 countries. The World Cup soccer finals were watched by three *billion* TV viewers.

CAUTION

No question that there are global brands—but are there global consumers? A 1990 world leadership study by the *Harvard Business Review* concluded:

"Change is indeed everywhere—regardless of country, culture, or corporation. But the idea of a corporate global village is more dream than reality."

The Economist questions whether the creation of a single market in Europe will lead to a convergence of consumer tastes. "Do not believe it until you see it," is the conclusion.

"Marketing and advertising folk have been busy hyping their latest creation: the euro-consumer. If you believe some of the puffs, there could soon be 320 million of these euro-clones, drinking euro-beer, eating euro-wurst and watching euro-soaps on euro-satellite television. To seasoned retailers, all this sounds like euro-baloney."

Which campaigns need to be aimed at *national* markets? Which can transcend borders for *global* or *regional* marketing?

MOVING IDEAS ACROSS BORDERS

Success in global marketing stems from a product or positioning that is relevant to consumer needs. Those needs will vary by culture.

Some products are not highly culture bound and are easier to market around the world—computers or consumer electronics, for example. Foods are more difficult, and the closer a particular food comes to being part of one country's staple diet, the harder it is to transfer across borders. One of the easier categories to market globally, according to Unilever, is an impulse product—like ice cream bars. Recognize cultural differences and be sensitive to them. Products may have to be modified to compete locally; McDonald's added beer to their menus in Germany.

While cultures and habits do vary, people's emotions are surprisingly similar, and that is what makes global brands possible.

Hallmark markets thousands of greeting cards, which address people's emotions. In a test, the top ten cards in the U.S. were identical to the top ten in England and, with one exception, in the same rank order.

People are very much alike regarding love, hate, fear, greed, envy, joy, patriotism, pornography, material comforts, and family. The way in which we touch those emotions may differ from country to country. Britons for example, are embarrassed by overt emotional appeals, whereas Americans and Australians are not.

British Telecom uses humor to promote phone calls. In the U.S., AT&T unabashedly urges, "Reach out and touch someone."

Some groups share cross-cultural identities more than others. "Japanese engineers or German teenagers are not 'foreigners,' " observes Peter Drucker. "They have the same tastes, values, and buying habits as American engineers or American teenagers."

Cross-cultural marketing may or may not mean the same advertising in each market.

HOW TO CREATE WORLDWIDE CAMPAIGNS

Worldwide advertising and global brands require three key ingredients:

■ Agreement on *international* or *regional* brand positioning, image and strategy.

■ *Local* understanding of the business environment and of national language, values, and culture.

■ A *shared* advertiser-agency commitment to the concept of a global brand.

Advertisers must be committed—with a corporate structure and philosophy—to make it happen. The agency cannot do it alone.

1. Think worldwide, not "international." There is a difference.

> *Procter & Gamble thinks of everything it does, including development of products, in terms of the entire world rather than as a U.S. export business. With this philosophy, P&G has built several world brands—Oil of Olay skin care, Always feminine care, 2-in-1 shampoo (Pert in the U.S.), and Pampers disposable diapers (50 percent market share in Europe).*

The first thing to agree upon is a world strategy for the products or services to be offered. While there will often be variations, a brand has to stand for something. Broad variations in the product line dilute the image of a brand and cannot be permitted, even if it means passing up a local business opportunity.

2. Agree upon an umbrella strategy for the brand, including positioning and brand personality. A strong global positioning signifies that a brand means the same thing to consumers in all countries.

> *The Guinness Stout campaign moves around the world with an enigmatic man dressed in black, playing off the beverage's dark color and embodying the brand personality*

of individualism. With quirky comments to appeal to a young audience, he walks past an abstract painting of a Guinness in one commercial and says, "If you don't get it, watch my lips," as he raises a glass. In Singapore, a well-known Chinese actor promotes the brand (in English, Mandarin, and Cantonese) with the wit and wisdom of a Chinese proverb—"I honor the past, I revere the future, but there is no time like the present"—as he smiles and drinks.

Keep the messages consistent. If the brand stands for high quality and premium price in one market, it simply cannot go after the low end in another.

The images in Philadelphia Brand cream cheese advertising vary substantially from country to country, but consumers everywhere identify it as the cream cheese with the smooth taste.

There will be times when a different strategy seems better for a local market situation. That is not a local decision. That is a *business* decision, with trade-offs that need to be examined. No work should be initiated on any alternate strategy without explicit, written approval from headquarters.

3. Capture knowledge from experience. It is important to develop and articulate principles, and set directions for creative execution. Put what you've learned into papers and presentations. Include an example of advertising that usually works—or doesn't—and explain why.

General Foods first introduced Tang outside the U.S. as a substitute for breakfast orange juice. Since the world was not making orange juice part of breakfast, Tang was successfully repositioned as a good-tasting, nutritious "space age" beverage used by astronauts.

Make sure everyone sees and understands the philosophy. Build it into indoctrination sessions for new people and training sessions for *all* people.

4. Encourage local initiative. Start with the proposition that there is a tested campaign as the standard, but allow alternative campaigns to be developed on the same strategy if market conditions warrant. But the principle must be that the alternate has to beat the control—not the reverse. The burden of proof is on the challenger.

> *Shell introduced an improved motor oil with a worldwide positioning: "Helix—the living oil." The campaign in Europe was a play on a hospital emergency room, with the car getting Helix as its treatment (the "lifeline for cars"). The campaign in Southeast Asia showed a crouching man rising out of the earth, being transformed into a car, and coming to life with the addition of Helix.*

Even a universally appealing strategy and style can be supplemented with market-specific promotions.

> *In Germany, the Marlboro Adventure Team competition appeals to German interest in American-style adventuring. In Malaysia and Indonesia, Marlboro sponsors badminton competitions; throughout Latin America, horse racing; and in Argentina, polo.*

Not all ideas have to come from the major advertising centers in New York or London; there's a lot of talent waiting to be tapped around the world.

5. Know the language. Proper use of language is vital. Be careful with translations and adaptations.

An advertisement headlined "Out of sight, out of mind" ran in Hungary. As translated, it read, "Invisible idiot."

Chevrolet changed the name of its Nova in Spain, since Nova in Spanish means "no go."

Pan-European commercials are now running that use the same visual, with only the voice-over changed for satellite transmission to different countries.

6. Know the culture. Different people have different values—in the foods they eat, the clothes they wear, in their relationships with each other.

In Japan, the Marlboro Man is always riding a white horse—to indicate he is a gentleman.

7. Think direct marketing. Mail and telephone are increasingly available around the world and should be a consideration in any plan.

Harrod's, the London-based retailer, advertises in a New York newspaper and offers to accept toll-free international telephone orders <u>from</u> the U.S. and provide quick delivery <u>to</u> the U.S.

International direct marketing is not as easy as within the U.S., with its one official language, one currency, one national postal service, one major telephone service, unlimited access to broadcast and print media, and the right to retain and use data. But it can be done.

8. Make it easy. Create a strong idea and format that can be easily adapted for worldwide use.

Pepsi talked an international language with a rock concert and a recognized star, Tina Turner. Several variations were produced for regional use. Brazilian and Mexican stars sang on stage with Tina—in their own language— for commercials to be used in Latin America. Individual countries were able to localize the campaign even further, by filming inserts with national favorites, making it appear they were on stage with Tina.

It is not always necessary to force other countries to completely reshoot advertising to be used locally. Consider formats like vignettes that make it easy to retain some scenes, shoot local adaptations for others, or create new ones for local use only. Consider formats where the picture tells the story and only the sound track needs to be changed.

9. Create and produce the advertising locally. It is crucial to understand national attitudes and habits, as well as language.

A couple impulsively decide to extend their romantic vacation on a warm island—this was the U.S. version; in the version for airing in Hong Kong, the more appropriate destination became Rome.

Global campaigns are created and produced locally, within an international vision.

THE MEDIA SCENE

"In the global village, read the local paper" is how The Economist *promotes itself to business readers.*

Advertising spending as a percent of gross national product is growing worldwide. Television is broadly available almost everywhere, but the typical household outside the U.S. still has few viewing choices. Government control of broadcasting in many countries has limited the development of broadcast stations. Although that is changing and TV advertising spending is increasing, print is the dominant medium in most countries. Magazines and newspapers provide a wide range of reading choices; as in the U.S., they are increasingly aimed at special interests and life-styles.

For some time, several U.S. magazines have printed pan-European editions in English. Now even more publishers are starting or adding local language editions, reports *The Wall Street Journal* (which itself has successfully established *The Wall Street Journal Europe* and *The Asian Wall Street Journal* editions).

"Publishers' interest in Europe today is tied to experts' predictions that a bigger advertiser pool lies within national borders than Europe-wide, despite the hoopla over the European Community's move to a single market by 1992 and the fall of political barriers in Eastern Europe."

Publishers are moving . . . cautiously.

REINVENTING THE WHEEL

A common focus cannot be accomplished by shipping an advertising campaign around the world.

An experienced internationalist once observed that the most common mistake in international marketing is to start by saying, "Now let's not let them reinvent the wheel." This attitude sounds right but fails, due to a lack of understanding about how the process works.

If you create the perfect wheel and send it out to be used, people will find a way to make it fail. They start with something like "It won't run on these roads." They will put it on the wrong vehicle, or forget to fill it with air. They will find a way to make it not work.

Better to take a different approach, and say, "We have come up with something circular that seems to work. Here are the plans, and here's the name of the inventor. Why don't you find a way to make it work in your country." Successful internationalists have learned the most important truth in international marketing:

The wheel that works best is the wheel people think they invented themselves.

12 Target Marketing

Technology is changing marketing. With more data on consumer habits and preferences, segmented media and data bases, *precision marketing* is increasingly possible: marketing aimed at specific segments or even individuals. The benefit: less waste and a more personalized message.

For many products and services, there will always be a need for marketing to mass audiences. However, no longer is it necessary to use mass media to reach smaller, more defined targets.

Some market targets are defined by demographics, others by attitude.

ATTITUDINAL SEGMENTS

Many product categories have distinct user groups that can be segmented by attitude. Car buyers, for example, have been divided by J. D. Power & Associates into six groups: functionalists, epicures, gearheads, purists, negatives, and road haters.

Gearheads typically spend weekends tinkering in the garage, rebuilding the car's high-powered engine; they tend to buy sporty cars. A road hater's first consideration in buying a car is safety.

New segmentations, such as by people's attitudes toward environmental issues and products, constantly emerge.

An important element of precision marketing is matching attitudes toward products and services, with attitudes in society. Trend spotter Jane Fitzgibbon has identified several major attitudinal segments.

The New Achievers New immigrant groups are changing the population composition of the U.S.; in five states, minorities make up more than 30 percent of the population. Because of new technology, the blue-collar worker has become a new kind of high-tech work force—the electric blue–collar worker. The fastest-growing well-paid occupations in the U.S. are computer operators, medical assistants, electronics technicians, and other "electric blues."

Don't expect these new affluents to adopt existing up-market consumer styles. They will create their own distinctive life-styles not necessarily characterized by the old symbols of achievement.

"Experience," says Fitzgibbon, "is becoming more important than possessions. Symbols of the good life, like the BMW and Cuisinart, are giving way to indulgences like travel and home services."

The Time Seekers As a society becomes more affluent, its time becomes more precious.

Now, as most workers' incomes have stagnated, leisure time is even more of a concern. A survey by the Roper Organization shows that only 47 percent of Americans feel they have enough leisure time—down from 60 percent in 1975. Families with two working parents particularly feel the problem, but many others are making tough choices between more money and more time.

"People are now saying they are willing to give up current income for leisure time, and that is a big change," says an associate professor of economics at Harvard. "A shift in materialistic values is taking place."

Increasingly, people will pay a premium for goods and services that give them time—car phones, fax machines, dog walkers, lawn care services, and home shopping by phone and catalog.

The New Age of Age This market is as much a state of mind as it is one of chronology.

Today's senior citizens are nothing like the grandparents of the last generation. They are thinking younger; living longer, healthier, and more dynamic lives; and are often starting second careers. Most of these seniors see themselves as 10 to 15 years younger than their chronological age.

A typical issue of *Modern Maturity*, the magazine of the American Association of Retired People, features articles on going back to school and 17 ways to win at tennis, in addition to tips on estate planning.

Don't isolate senior citizens from the rest of the population in advertising, and don't show them as infirm, sexless, ill, or lonely. Show them with younger friends too, remind them you know they can be active, and let them select products (like low-sodium foods) that meet their needs. Give them a vigorous self-portrait in advertising.

Life Simplifiers The ever increasing proliferation of choices in consumer goods, technologies, and media is creating a whirl of confusion and stress. Too much choice leads to services that help consumers make the right one: TV and movie critics to help decide what to watch, in-store fashion consultants, consumer reports on products, and other informational support.

Branded products and services bring the added value of simplification through assurance of quality and other benefits.

> *"Consumers like brands because they package meaning,"* *writes Alex Biel, head of the Ogilvy Center for Research &* *Development. "They form a kind of shorthand that makes* *choice easier. They let me escape from a feature-by-feature* *analysis of category alternatives."*

Premium Brand Consumers Once the province of just the well-to-do, premium products are now for everyone. It's due as much to increased sophistication as to affluence. Consider the secretary with the Gucci bag or Hermes scarf. Attitudinal segmentation like this is hard to target but attractive as a market.

In almost all categories, premium products emerge, often followed by superpremium brands. These are valuable assets, created by nontraditional marketing and advertising, aimed at people who want to set themselves apart from the crowd.

Premium brands start with quality, not snob appeal. They seldom start with advertising, which is often the last part of the marketing program.

> *The launch of Henry Weinhard's Private Reserve, the best-selling superpremium beer in the Northwest, started with a specially brewed product—and word-of-mouth advertising. The product was introduced at selected bars, and the bartender was given the facts about the product quality. Only after word started to spread was it distributed in selected stores, and only when its reputation had grown was it introduced into supermarkets, with advertising.*

It is crucial to understand the psychology of what people look for in premium products in order to create effective advertising. Selling prestige is a fast way to fail; understatement is the better strategy.

> *The great success of Jack Daniel's premium sour mash whiskey is based on a theory: "the illusion of discovery." Like finding a great fishing spot, discovering a product nobody else knows about gives people a great deal of satisfaction. Advertising for Jack Daniel's is almost recessive—black-and-white photos, small headlines, no holiday decanters or testimonials, understated copy.*

When enough people discover the brand, it can be rewarding. Class becomes mass.

DEMOGRAPHIC SEGMENTS

The major growth segments in the U.S. are minority groups such as Hispanics, blacks, and Asian-Americans.

The 1990 census found that one in four Americans is now of non-European descent.

Several of the largest cosmetics companies acknowledged the growing nonwhite population by introducing products for darker-skinned people. Deeper Tones of Almay is promoted by advertising in English and Spanish.

Two other major segments—women and children—also require special consideration in advertising, and this section will comment on them as well.

Hispanics A large and rapidly growing market, over 20 million people, the Hispanic community could be the largest minority group by the year 2000. It is concentrated in large cities in three regions: the Mexican-American population in the Southwest and Southern California, the Cuban community in southern Florida, and the Puerto Rican and Dominican communities in New York, the Northeast, and Chicago.

Local merchants—supermarkets, car dealers, furniture stores, doctors, lawyers—were the first to discover the need to communicate to this market in its first language, Spanish, and the payoff of doing so.

Hispanics are very brand loyal. They watch TV and listen to radio more than they buy newspapers or magazines, and they respond best to Hispanic advertising in Hispanic programming, using ethnic casting (but not stereotypes).

Accents and speech patterns vary, but Hispanics all use the same Spanish language dictionary.

Blacks (or African-Americans) "Black people are not dark-skinned white people," says Tom Burrell of Burrell Communications. "Blacks are significantly different in terms of approach—our history, how we came here, how we developed as citizens. There is a significant difference in behavior, and that manifests itself all the way to the marketplace."

The first principle of black advertising: *make it believable*. It is the *little* things that make a difference. The casting, the language, what the actors are wearing in a commercial can make a difference between one that hits home or one that is a turnoff.

At the same time, there is a different culture. Advertising in the black community has some similarities to taking a campaign to another country; it should be created and produced by people who know the "language," the market, and the culture.

The second principle: *don't insult people's intelligence*. Don't patronize or use stereotypes. An all-white commercial in black media is not just missing a business opportunity; it is insulting. Advertising with a single black actor or actress in an otherwise all-white commercial is obvious tokenism. Situations that are not part of a black life-style irritate people and can backfire.

Use minority talent to reach a minority target, and accurately represent the population mix.

Asian-Americans The Asian-American community is not one but several—Chinese, Japanese, Koreans, Filipinos, Vietnamese, and so on—each speaking a different language. In addition, there are Indians and Pakistanis from the Asian subcontinent.

It may be difficult to talk to this market, but it is worth the effort. The growth rate alone makes it hard to ignore; it doubled in the '80s and could grow another 40 percent in the '90s. Compared to the total U.S. population, Asian-Americans are more affluent, better educated, and are better represented in management and the professions.

The problem is this community's absolute size—at seven million, not the smallest but not as large or homogeneous as many. The solution is not a single one or a simplistic one. Avoid trying to talk to everyone at once, and avoid stereotypes (exotic-looking women and dragons). Capture nuances.

Women A decade after the start of the women's movement, it became fashionable to single out women as targets with special marketing devices.

■ Hotels fitted rooms in pink and white and reserved them for women only. Women refused to stay in them.

■ Banks set up special Women's Services Departments and headlined ads "Career Girls!" Women refused to bank with them; almost all these special departments closed down.

Treat women as consumers. That's what they are.

They—especially working women—respond to ideas that will save them time. They respond more than men to emotional appeals, but don't single them out in the advertising as irrational airheads.

They want to be treated as people, not stereotypes. "Helen Homemaker," Jane Fitzgibbon reminds advertisers, "is no more an absolute reality than is Betty Briefcase."

Children Marketing to children involves first a shared sense of responsibility between the advertiser and the parent. The American Academy of Pediatrics policy statement on children's television says, "Parents must educate children to become responsible and informed consumers."

Some of the regulation of children's advertising has eased; the responsibility remains.

Children are heavy viewers of television. They watch more *adult* television than children's television, according to Nielsen. TV is an especially pervasive medium among children under 10.

The market is not one, but three: the one-to-five-year-old preschoolers rely most on parental decisions; the six-to-nine-year-olds are faddists, and the heaviest watchers of television; the 10-to-13-year-olds emulate teenagers.

It is especially important not to distort a product's appearance or performance, not to suggest making friends is a reason to use a product, and not to encourage eating habits that could interfere with good nutrition.

Advertising to children can be effective *and* socially responsible. Children are a special audience, and there are principles of effective communication:

■ *Make the product fun and the advertising funny.*
The zanier and broader, the better.

In the Flintstones campaign for Pebbles cereal, Barney constantly finds inventive ways to trick Fred into giving up his good-tasting cereal. The kids all know what's going to happen—and they love it.

■ *Children like reality.*
They can relate to things that grow out of their own experience: slumber parties for girls; hand-clapping games for young children. They like the action and excitement of video games, which simulate reality.

■ *Create a personality for the product.*

It will keep kids loyal, and they won't easily be persuaded to switch.

> *The world's largest-selling fashion doll, Barbie, helps little girls live out their fantasies with aspirational products and advertising and remains a leader by staying current with contemporary life-styles. Barbie's black counterpart is Shani.*

■ *Music is key.*

At all ages, it is a universal language. Kids know the videos, and they love to dance. Contemporary rock music with a strong beat is what they like, not corny or old-fashioned tunes.

■ *Be careful with casting.*

Children emulate older children. When in doubt, cast older. Girls emulate boys, but boys don't emulate girls. When in doubt, cast boys (at least for unisex products). Boys respond best to action and excitement. Both boys and girls respond to kindness and friendship.

Watch and listen to children, and talk to them in terms of *their* experience, not your memories of childhood. They have computers in schools and are very comfortable with technology. They are aware of TV at a younger age than ever before. They are growing up much faster, are more sophisticated, and can tell when someone is trying to manipulate them.

Today children are assuming household responsibilities, and they contribute to some family purchase decisions—even those regarding VCRs and vacation destinations. But don't forget to reassure parents about a product (in separate advertising) when appropriate.

The Kool-Aid Pitcherman talks to kids in their own terms; separate advertising to mothers talks about vitamin C.

The Children's Advertising Review unit of the Council of Better Business Bureaus has helpful guidelines for advertising to children.

One of the most powerful trends in American society is the growing importance of market segments. Stunning advances in technology and media enable advertisers to talk more directly to individuals or groups in terms of their specific interests, and as a result, marketing is achieving a new level of precision.

13 Truth and Ethics

THERE ARE THINGS we do in advertising because they are the law, and things we do because they are right.

What is *truthful* is clearly determined by the law. What is *right* is a matter of corporate conscience. Advertisers have extralegal responsibilities, and they need to take these just as seriously as they do legal ones.

ADVERTISING AND THE LAW

Much of the federal legislation that regulates advertising started when the Federal Trade Commission was created by Congress in 1914 to deal with "deceptive and unfair acts and practices in commerce."

The FTC isn't the only agency that polices advertising. Over 30 statutes allow others to scrutinize advertising as well—the Food and Drug Administration for food, drugs, and cosmetics, the U.S. Postal Service for mailed advertising materials, the Federal Communications Commission for radio and television advertising, and the Securities and Exchange Commission for stocks and bonds advertising, among others.

States also get into the act, and the National Association of State Attorneys General is increasingly active.

Here are some basic legal rules:

1. Tell the truth, show the truth. Your product must be shown exactly as the consumer buys it in all *material* respects. You cannot have a product specially selected or constructed for use in advertising. Take it right off the production line. If the dessert melts under the hot camera lights, that's too bad; you cannot tamper with it to make it firmer. If the dog won't eat the dog food, that's too bad; under no conditions can you doctor it to get the dog to eat.

This is particularly true of demonstrations.

> *Television and print ads showed a Volvo withstanding the impact of a giant-tired truck that flattened other cars. It was later found that the Volvo's roof had been reinforced, while the support of some of the other cars had been weakened. Although the Volvo was strong enough to hold the weight, this was seen as a misrepresentation of a material fact. The advertising was withdrawn, and both the advertiser and agency were fined by the Federal Trade Commission.*

Packages can be cleaned up to reproduce better, things that don't impinge on product performance can be touched up, but the product is inviolate.

> *Glasses in a beer advertisement cannot be retouched to make the beer appear lighter or darker. A blemish on the beer drinker's cheek—which is not material to the sale of the product—can be retouched. A blemish on a woman's cheek in a skin care advertisement is material, however, and cannot be retouched.*

Avoid strange camera angles that make the product look other than it is or unusual props, such as a smaller-than-normal cereal bowl to make a portion look larger than normal.

2. Make the general impression truthful. The advertising will be judged not by what it says, but by what the consumer *thinks* it says.

> *A food product together with an eight-ounce glass of milk adds up to a nutritionally balanced meal; if the consumer receives the impression that the product is complete by itself, even if the milk is mentioned or shown, the advertising is deceptive.*

If research indicates consumers are getting the wrong *impression*, correct it. Otherwise the FTC can rule that the advertising is deliberately intended to deceive.

Disclaimers need not be dull.

> *A commercial for a Roy Rogers promotion depicts a concerned father asking his prospective son-in-law how the couple plans to eat. On learning the answer, "Bacon cheeseburgers from Roy's," the father remarks, "Surely, you don't plan to eat bacon cheeseburgers for the rest of your life?" "Relax. No sweat," the young man replies. "It's a limited-time offer."*

3. Ban "weasels" and dangling comparisons. "This detergent can give you the whitest wash you've ever seen." The weasel is *can*, which the consumer is likely to miss.

"This detergent will give you a whiter wash." That's a dangling comparison. Whiter than what? A whiter wash than the detergent used to, or a whiter wash than the competition does?

Make it clear.

4. Substantiate product claims. There are subjective claims about a product that cannot be substantiated—a beautiful carpet, great-tasting potato chips, "fried chicken like Mother used to make." Then there are objective or competitive claims—more durable than the other leading carpet, chips that stay crisp after the bag is opened. For these, you must have high-quality research or evidence that the claim is true, and you must be able to prove that a majority of consumers think the claim is correct.

5. Back testimonials with research. Several consumers may be convinced that your product does things better than anything else on the market and may be willing to say so on television. That's not enough.

- *You need evidence that the product will in fact do what these people say it will do.*

- *These people must represent a majority of consumers, not just an aberrational few.*

- *They must have come to these views before "consideration" was involved; that is, before they knew there was a possibility of being paid.*

If celebrities endorse the product, they must have been using it *before* being approached—and be able to prove it; they must continue to use it as long as the campaign runs.

Who Is Responsible? The advertiser and the advertising agency are separately and equally liable for advertising presented to the consumer. The advertiser cannot take on the entire responsibility and absolve the agency of liability.

Each is considered especially knowledgeable in areas of its own expertise. The advertiser is responsible for providing accurate product information, which the agency (without its own technical research facilities) can rely on as truth. The agency, on its part, is responsible for truthful photography of the product, accurate documentation of demonstrations, and substantiation of testimonials.

Don't take anything for granted. Both agency and advertiser should be represented at preproduction meetings and on the set of any production where a question might arise.

ADVERTISING AND RESPONSIBILITY

The first responsibility is to protect the consumer, by telling people what they need to know in order to make an informed choice.

More information about products and services, with some sensible limits, is clearly in the public interest; nutritional information on foods and ingredient disclosures on proprietary medicines, for example. The place to start is on the package itself, with more informative labeling.

Advertising Review Boards Many companies have set up advertising review boards to make sure they live up to the highest standards of law and responsibility. The purpose of these boards is to ensure that all marketing and communications programs are truthful, clear, and in good taste, and to guard against consumer misinterpretation. They also act as a kind of internal audit to substantiate advertising claims.

It is particularly important to set down standards for

media, including which television programs or magazines are or are not appropriate. Special-interest pressure groups are prone to use threats of boycotts to influence media selections, and advertisers can be whipsawed if standards have not been established in advance.

Privacy The use of what people consider private information is of growing concern to consumer advocates, legislators, and the media. It grows with the ever increasing availability of consumer data and the ability to manage information. The issue is whether people are informed and consent to having their names used for certain purposes.

You may not be able to ask for information about an individual, but you can ask for lists of people who have certain characteristics in common, whether it be gender, amount of income, type of residence, or buying habits.

The New York Times observes, "Data bases of people's spending habits are simply too attractive a marketing tool." When Citicorp announced a plan to give marketing access to its files on 21 million credit-card customers, a potential gold mine for target marketing, a Citicorp Visa card holder protested:

> *"They know a lot about me and my buying habits, and there's a lot of knowledge there I'd be extremely upset to have disclosed. There's a quantum leap between Citicorp using that information for Citicorp things and them offering it to people I've never had a relationship with— and, in all statistical likelihood, never will."*

Many products and services simply would not exist without the free flow of personal customer data. The object is to maintain a balance between these needs and the need to protect consumer privacy.

> *"Where do we draw the line?" asks consumerist Meredith Layer. "How do we balance all of the public, government and consumer advocate concerns about privacy with our dependency on the use of personal data in many businesses? What steps must we take now to ensure that we continue to control our own destiny on the issue of privacy?"*

Marketers must accept the principle of "informed consent." Rules are needed so that people know what information about them is on file and how it may be used, so that they know they have the right to "opt out." Awareness on the issue must be raised, and internal safeguards set up to ensure procedures are being followed.

Public Service Advertising One of the great contributions of the advertising business is the use of its talents for community and social causes.

The Partnership for a Drug-Free America, a coalition of volunteer agencies, created a series of campaigns on the many faces of drug abuse.

> *An egg being dropped into a frying pan illustrates the powerful headline, "This is your brain on drugs."*

> *Another advertisement shows a teenager with the barrel of a revolver pointed up his nose. The headline: "Cocaine."*

Most public service advertising has been channeled through the Advertising Council, which was founded to help mobilize the country in World War II and continued thereafter to take on such causes as drunk-driving prevention, fighting pollution, and preventing forest fires.

Smokey the Bear has been working to reduce forest fires for nearly 50 years.

"A mind is a terrible thing to waste," the long-running campaign for the United Negro College Fund, has helped raise over $700 million for historically black colleges, enabling several hundred thousand students to receive college educations.

Advertising Council president Ruth Wooden describes the organization as the most visible example of business volunteerism at work. "I'm not trying to be dramatic when I say that some decisions are life-and-death decisions," says Wooden. "By the nature of what we can accomplish, we have to select issues where advertising can make a difference."

To make a difference, public service advertising must be just as disciplined and professional as commercial advertising. It must answer questions like:

■ **Is advertising the best way to do the job?** There are advantages and disadvantages to advertising. Maybe other kinds of communication, like public relations, would be better or cheaper.

■ **What is the best way to get the media involved?** The first audience is the media. Broadcasters and publishers are bombarded by organizations asking for free time and space. They can't run everything.

■ **What are the objectives and strategy?** The most effective advertising campaigns, public service or any other kind, have one message and one image that they stay with year after year after year.

- **What is the reader or viewer being asked to do?** There may be a call to action (an 800 phone number) or an attempt to change behavior (putting out a campfire, cutting down fat in a diet, voting).

> *Advertising by the World Wildlife Fund to convince people of the need to conserve Amazonian rain forests closes with "World Wildlife Fund, Rain Forest Rescue Campaign. 1-800-CALL-WWF."*

- **How will it be measured?** Accountability must be measured in numbers, not just emotions.

Public service advertising, if disciplined and targeted, works.

> *An Ad Council study with the Advertising Research Foundation found that TV commercials persuaded double the number of men to get screening tests for colon cancer, which increased the survival rate from 50 percent to over 90 percent.*

Political Advertising There are few more emotionally charged subjects than this one. Some groups want to ban it entirely; others point to fundamental First Amendment issues. As currently practiced, it casts all advertising in a bad light.

Political leaders must use contemporary media to communicate and lead, as well as to get elected, and orations are no longer the way to communicate to a mass audience.

It is reasonable to insist that political advertising be both fair and true. There is a fine line between regulation and censorship of free speech, but it is around this issue that the debate should be engaged. Unlike product advertising, where the consumer just doesn't buy again if dissatisfied, political advertising leaves voters stuck with a choice that affects their lives over the long term.

Green Marketing The growing concern for the environment is reflected in marketing, with the issue being exploited by some. The FTC and state attorneys general are working on advertising guidelines for terms like *biodegradable*, *recyclable*, and *environmentally friendly*.

Claims must be based on the existence of conditions broadly available; if a disposable diaper is promoted as biodegradable, there must be composting sites equipped to handle them in enough places in the country to make the claim true for most people. If the advertising uses the terms "recyclable" or "environmentally friendly," that means under all reasonable conditions.

Food Labeling "Fresh." "No Cholesterol." "Fat-free." "Light." "Low-calorie." These are some of the terms and claims under scrutiny by the Food and Drug Administration.

"We are shifting into an era where our responsibility is not only safety but accurate information about products," says FDA Commissioner David Kessler. "The integrity of the food label rests on one fundamental concept: that the information it provides is truthful—not false, and not misleading."

Food advertising will continue to be regulated by the FTC; the stricter FDA standards for food labels have implications for advertising as well.

REGULATION AND RESPONSIBILITY

Advertising is a high-profile medium. It comes into our homes and our lives, it reflects values and it attracts attention. While its purpose is to sell, it must also have a sense of social responsibility. Advertising does not exist in an amoral environment.

Unfortunately, advertising is a highly visible target. Its excesses of bad taste (use of sexuality, questionable stereotypes, loud appeals) have been criticized, many times with justification.

Criticism is often followed by threats of regulation. Advertising should be regulated by someone, and that someone is primarily the advertising industry, which must regulate itself, following the letter and the spirit of the law.

Advertisers need to be responsible in product labeling and advertising. Agencies must insist that clients give them substantiation for all product claims. Broadcasters, publishers, and educators must be part of the process. What is at stake is free speech and information. Consumers need to be able to choose, rather than having the choice made for them.

Tell the truth, the whole truth, and nothing but the truth.

14 Agency Relations

W HY IS IT that one client gets outstanding advertising from an agency, and another in the same agency gets less than brilliant work?

The advertising one gets from an agency depends in large part on the client.

A great relationship with an advertising agency is nurtured and built over time. Like a marriage, you have to work at it.

Create an environment for great ideas.

Nothing is more important, on both sides, than a fertile environment in which ideas can flourish. That starts with an understanding of the creative process.

There is a German expression, *fingerspitzen*, literally a feeling in the fingertips; managing ideas requires something like that, a special sensitivity. Managing creativity is an art.

■ **Protect new ideas.** Too many organizations are filled with well-meaning people who can kill ideas with questions. Or there may simply be so many organizational layers that the vitality is filtered out of ideas.

"The innovative company understands that innovation starts with an idea. And ideas are somewhat like babies— they are born small, immature, and shapeless."

—PETER DRUCKER

■ **Take risks.** Original means untried, and therefore entails risk. Ideas represent change, and sometimes scare organizations.

■ **Nurture creative people.** That doesn't mean coddling; it does mean encouraging and stimulating them.

■ **Separate ideas from idea-givers** —when you're being critical. Not "You really missed that one," but "That idea misses." When you praise, give by-lines.

Creativity is not just the job of the creative department. Everyone must want to work toward high creative goals.

HOW TO BE A BETTER CLIENT

1. Ask big questions. Aiming for greatness means asking for it. Ask big questions to get big answers. Let the agency know that you are confident that they will deliver more than good, solid advertising—and that you expect more.

2. Learn the fine art of conducting a creative meeting. Deal with the important issues first: strategy; consumer benefit; brand positioning and personality. State clearly whether you think the advertisement succeeds in these areas. And if not, why not. It drives agency people wild to push themselves hard to come up with a great campaign, only to have a client deal with just the details. It's okay to tell people they have missed the target; just don't let them sit there guessing.

3. Be human. Try to react like a person, not a corporation. When you like the advertising, let everyone know you like it. Send the copywriter a note; you may be amazed at the results. Be frank when you don't like the advertising. Just give people a reason why you are turning it down. (They may even agree.)

Be willing to admit you are not sure. You may need time to absorb what they've been thinking about and working on for weeks. Don't let anyone press you by asking for an approval immediately after a presentation of new work.

4. Be consistent. Tell people where you want to go. Set objectives, for your business and your advertising—and stick with them.

Insist upon a measure of creative discipline. Professionals don't bridle at discipline (nor did Shakespeare, who thrived within the discipline of the sonnet form).

5. Simplify the approval process. Presentations at several levels of an organization, often with slight variations in direction at each level, weaken ideas. Someone once described the process as being nibbled to death by ducks. You don't feel much pain, but you wake up one day and your leg is gone.

Beware of all those "little changes" that add up.

6. Make the agency feel responsible. Tell them what you think is wrong, not how to fix it. The best clients are not meddlers. Agencies work harder if someone points out the major problems, then lets them find the solution. If they expect someone always to tell them what to do, they won't try as hard on the original presentation.

7. Suggest work sessions. The time to get involved is early in the process. Informal give-and-take sessions, where people can discuss rough ideas, often help set the right direction early and save time later.

8. Stay in touch. With all the pressures of business, it is easy to become insular and narrow. You see the same people at the office and at home, and there isn't the time to break away.

Try to stay in touch with a changing market and a changing customer. Get into the field, visit stores, talk to buyers or store managers. Sit in on a few focus group sessions. Catch a cold and watch a day of television.

9. Keep agency people involved in your business. Tell them what's happening, good and bad—that includes the creative people; they want to know the latest market shares too. Your success is ultimately theirs.

10. Care about being a good client. Within an agency, the best people get to work on the best accounts. Otherwise, the agency cannot hold them.

Creative people do their best work for clients they like and respect. That doesn't mean easy clients.

Take advantage of the natural competition within an agency, and get the best people fighting to work on your advertising.

EVALUATING AN AGENCY

One of the most important ways to nurture the relationship is to tell people honestly what you think of them.

The process goes both ways.

At least once a year there should be a *formal* evaluation where both client and agency can openly discuss how to make the relationship better. Many issues will be discussed informally during the year, but this is no substitute for a written review.

It will necessarily be a review of both successes and shortcomings, of projects and people. But the best evaluations also look forward and set a short list of up to five major objectives. Review sessions during the year can then measure progress against these goals to determine what obstacles need to be removed and how to alter the objectives if needed.

This process eliminates the small irritations that creep into a relationship and helps keep everyone moving in the same direction.

AGENCY COMPENSATION

It is the agency's job to manage its profitability by controlling costs, not the advertiser's. The agency cannot control revenue, however, except in the way it prices its services and gets paid.

A profitable agency does better work, and profitable accounts within an agency attract better people. Word gets around fast; people don't want to tie their careers to marginal accounts.

There are many ways to pay an agency: commissions, fees, and commission-fee combinations. There is a growing interest in incentive compensation plans, which tie some part of the agency's pay to performance—sales targets, favorable changes in brand image in tracking studies, or specific projects or tasks.

Whatever the plan, it should embrace several principles:

■ **Incentives to build the client's business:** commissions on higher budgets; larger fees; bonuses for success.

■ **Incentives to the agency to control its costs.** Cost-plus systems are an incentive to be inefficient.

■ **A fair profit to the agency over time.** That doesn't mean a guaranteed profit. Agencies expect to invest for a year or so in start-ups or in tough times; they can't afford to invest year after year.

■ **A plan that is simple to administer.** You want to spend your time discussing advertising rather than compensation.

SELECTING AN AGENCY

Selecting an agency for a new assignment is one thing; firing one and choosing another is something else. Changing agencies is traumatic for everyone and not necessarily the best thing for the business.

If an agency has had a series of weak evaluations and has not moved vigorously to correct problems, if you've tried changing people *within* the agency, if there is a real reason for change (as opposed to the desire for a "fresh look"), then there is no alternative but to seek a new agency partner.

The process will be time-consuming, highly publicized, and at times confusing.

Some things you shouldn't be confused by:

- *Speculative campaigns.*

Frequently, agencies are asked—or even volunteer—to create new campaigns to win the business and to illustrate their thinking.

There is no guarantee that this advertising will work in the market; often it never even runs.

- *Size.*

Put aside the stereotypes that only small agencies are creative or that only the big agencies can handle big clients. The real issue is the team that is assigned to the business.

- *Conflicts.*

These are often overblown by the trade press. Conflicts are largely an emotional issue. We've never heard of any trade secrets being stolen; it's hard enough to get people to pay attention to the research and data at hand. Other professional service firms such as management consultants, lawyers, and accountants handle several clients in a category. Better to look the other way on tangential conflicts then to eliminate a strong agency by being a hardliner.

- *Creative awards.*

Recognize them for what they are—awards that the industry gives to itself. Awards are seldom given for sales. Judges tend to favor humor, special effects, advertising that is on the cutting edge in technique. Awards have a role in attracting talent and branding an agency as creative, but they should not be the primary criterion for selecting an agency.

Some things to consider:

■ *Define your needs.*

Put them in writing, and get agreement from all the key people who will have a say in the advertising. What special skills are needed? What is your policy on product conflicts?

■ *Make an agency short list.*

Pull together a list of agencies whose point of view you respect and who have an affinity for your business. People come and go; you need an organization with a business and creative philosophy, stable management, professional staff, technical expertise, and a past, present, and future.

■ *Select a few finalists.*

Visit the agencies on the list; lengthy questionnaires won't tell you what you need to know. Meet the people who will work on your business, as well as the principals. Spend time with them informally and individually, not just in conference rooms. Personal chemistry is important. Avoid new business teams who disappear after the presentation.

■ *Do some checking.*

What kind of reports do you get from other clients, from the media, from employees?

■ *Manage the presentation.*

Concentrate on presentations that show how an agency thinks, not how much show business can be put into them. Prohibit any finished creative work; concept boards with a strategy are usually enough. Do they talk about the strategy—or the execution? Make your own decision on an agency's ability to contribute to the marketing strategy and, within that, to develop effective advertising strategies.

At the end of the selection process, you must feel comfortable with the team. They should *know* your business, and you should feel they have the resources to deal with the tough problems. Then wait 24 hours and make a decision.

In a speech to the American Association of Advertising Agencies, John Pepper of Procter & Gamble said:

> *"I believe in advertising quite simply because I have seen throughout 25 years that the correlation between profitable—let me emphasize profitable—business growth on our brands and having great copy isn't 25 percent, it's not 50 percent, it's not 75 percent; it is 100 percent."*

A worthwhile goal for great advertising and a great partnership.

15 What It Takes to Succeed

Brains. Advertising is a fast-changing business, and it takes raw intelligence to digest a steady stream of new information. You can rise to a certain level on diligence and organization, but insightful thinking is needed to lead great advertising.

A creative feel. Advertising is different from most other businesses; its product is creative. That requires a special sensitivity to the process and an awareness of trends in entertainment and the arts. Go to movies, art museums, and concerts. Read books and magazines. Stay in touch with popular taste.

An inquiring mind. Study the market and the precedents. Observe what works and what doesn't—and find out why. Seek out trends that will have an impact. Find patterns and establish new principles. Be a student of the business.

A love of ideas. Do you create ideas? Do you get excited about finding solutions to problems? Advertising is a business of ideas, and everyone is expected to contribute. Don't wait for others—initiate. Push yourself to come up with ideas.

A sense of organization. Coming up with ideas is fun; knowing what to do with them is business. If you say you'll do something, do it. The saying around McKinsey & Company is, "Deliver on all promises, and make no promises on which you can't deliver."

The ability to write well. A lot of time and energy is wasted because people don't understand what they are expected to do. Learn to communicate clearly—in letters, memos, reports, and recommendations—and you'll be a step ahead.

The ability to persuade. Whether presenting a new strategy or a new campaign, it is critical that you are able to articulate a point of view clearly. You have to know how to sell.

Commitment. An idea is not an idea until it is sold. The people who accomplish things in advertising don't just come up with ideas; they relentlessly press them in every forum until they happen. They *never* give up if they think it is important.

Leadership. Many people are involved in creating advertising, and even more in an orchestrated campaign that involves the disciplines of direct marketing, sales promotion, and public relations. The ability to get people to work together toward a single goal is a rare but essential quality.

Resilience. There are long hours filled with changes and stress. It takes stamina to bounce back after disappointments and to be able to attack the problem with fresh energy.

Advertising is a marvelous business. Working with creative people is stimulating. The problems are challenging. The product is rewarding, and it works.

Many are attracted to advertising without understanding what it takes to succeed. The list of qualities above may seem daunting, but the people who rise to the top have most of them—plus one other.

Motivation. Do you *sincerely* want to succeed?

Glossary

Adlobs: Ad-like objects, used in creative testing, are more than an unadorned concept or benefit statement, but less than an advertisement.

Ad-Tel: A marketing service based chiefly on store scanning data.

Airbrush retouching: A little cylinder (an airbrush) sprays watercolor paint over a halftone to correct error or add effects. (This technique is being replaced by **electronic retouching**.)

AM station: A radio station that broadcasts through its amplitude or power rather than its frequency. An AM station can broadcast further but is received with more static and interference.

Animatics: A technique for testing less expensive versions of television commercials by producing film or tape of the drawings on the storyboard. In **photomatics**, photographs are used instead of drawings.

Area of Dominant Influence (ADI):	A geographical television market as defined by Arbitron. Every county is assigned to only one ADI based on where its highest share of viewing occurs. Similar to **DMA**.
Artwork or art:	Any visual, whether a drawing or photograph, used in a print advertisement. **Line art** is a drawing or other visual that has no tonal values, so it can be printed without use of a halftone screen. **Tone art** usually means a photograph.
Audio:	The written description on a storyboard of what the viewer hears during the commercial, including spoken words, sound effects and music.
Benefit:	Key consumer rationale.
Bleed:	An illustration that runs right off the page, with no border. **Nonbleed** advertisements have a white border around them.
Brand:	The *name* of a product; a set of added values.
Brand Development Index (BDI):	A measurement of a product's percentage of sales as a ratio (brand sales divided by population).
Brand image:	The personality of a brand.
Bullets:	A graphic device, usually dots, stars or squares.

Campaign: A series of advertisements held together by visual similarities, verbal similarities or a similarity of attitude.

Caption: Description of what is in a photograph or drawing, most commonly placed beneath it.

Category: A class of goods or services.

Category Development Index (CDI): A measurement of a class of product sales as a ratio. (Category sales divided by population.)

Cause-related marketing: Linking the sale of a product or service with the support of a good cause.

Cinema verite: A commercial style borrowed from film documentaries, it uses a hand-held camera and natural lighting.

Circulation: The number of copies of a magazine or newspaper that are distributed in any given issue.

Claim: Statement about the performance of a product or service. A **competitive** or **objective claim** must be based upon research, laboratory testing or other factual evidence. A **subjective claim** does not need support.

Closing date: For print media, the final date to commit to the purchase of advertising space.

Communications testing:	Research to determine whether your advertising is saying the right thing.
Composition:	Percentage of a medium's total audience that is part of a specific demographic segment.
Computer imaging:	A computer generates visuals that are then printed on paper.
Concept testing:	Research that helps determine how a product should be positioned.
Confidence level:	A measure of the probability that research results would be the same if carried out again.
Consumer promotion:	Incentives for the consumer to buy the product.
Control:	A proven winner against which all new mailings or advertisements are tested.
Conversion rate:	Cost of moving a prospect from inquiry to purchase.
Cost per inquiry (CPI):	Cost of a mailing divided by the number of responses.
Cost per point (CPP):	Cost to buy a rating point.
Cost per thousand (CPM):	Cost to reach 1,000 members of a target audience.
Coverage:	Degree to which a media vehicle is able to reach an audience.

Crop:	To move in on one area of a photograph or drawing and eliminate the rest.
Curriculum marketing:	A sequence of timed mailings to a particular target.
Cut:	Rapid transition from one film scene to another.
Cutout:	Addition to the surface of a billboard that may be three-dimensional.
Data base:	A list that goes beyond names and addresses and includes demographic and psychographic information.
Daypart:	Defined time periods of the broadcast day used for analytical purposes.
Demographics:	Descriptive facts about a given population group—household income, education, age, sex.
Demonstration:	Visual proof that the product or service does what is claimed.
Designated Market Area (DMA):	A geographical television market as defined by Nielsen. Similar to **ADI**.
Die cut:	Hole that appears in a printed page as intentional part of the design.
Display allowance:	Money given to the retailer by the manufacturer in return for space to put up a display.

Dissolve: A slow transition from one shot to another, usually to denote passage of time.

Downtest: Creating a less expensive marketing package by dropping one or more elements, and testing it against the control.

Duplication: Percentage of people that see the message in more than one media or publication. In direct marketing, appearance of the same name on more than one mailing list.

DV (Direct Voice): Indication on a storyboard that someone is speaking "on camera."

Dye transfer: Process of transferring a color transparency to special paper so it can be retouched. (This technique is being replaced by **electronic retouching**.)

Electronic retouching: The photographer's original image is scanned into a computer system; picture elements are then manipulated to achieve the effects of retouching.

FCC (Federal Communications Commission): Agency that regulates broadcasters.

FDA (Food and Drug Administration): Agency that regulates advertising of foods, drugs and cosmetics.

Fiber optic cable:	Thin glass fibers are bundled together in cables to transmit digital information by means of light pulses.
Flighting:	The concentration of advertising into bursts, with a period of no advertising in between.
FM station:	A radio station that broadcasts by modifying its frequency, resulting in high fidelity in reception.
Focus group session:	A group of people selected from a target audience, led by a skilled moderator, express their attitudes about a product, service or general topic of interest.
Four color process:	Four separate plates of the same photograph are prepared, in red, yellow, blue, and black. The combination of these four colors reproduces a facsimile of the original photograph.
Frequency:	Number of times the message is potentially seen or heard in a defined period of time.
Frequency distribution:	The exact number of times individuals are exposed to advertising in a schedule.
FSI (Free standing insert):	A separate printed piece with advertisements and coupons, usually delivered within a newspaper.

FTC (Federal Trade Commission):	Agency that enforces truth in advertisements.
Gatefold:	The extension to a page in a magazine that can be unfolded or opened.
Geo-demographic systems:	Sophisticated data bases that store information on population groups.
Gross impressions:	Total number of messages delivered by a media plan.
Gross Rating Points (GRPs):	Total of all rating points achieved for a specific schedule or campaign.
Halftone:	An illustration that shows lights and shadows by means of tiny dots.
Hiatus:	A period in which an advertiser runs no advertising.
Hidden camera:	A technique borrowed from commercial television. Participants are filmed by a camera hidden from them.
High ground:	In most categories, one benefit more meaningful than any other.
Hot spots:	Places in a catalog or letter that attract extra readership.
HUT:	Percentage of Households Using Television at any given time.
Inbound:	The use of 800 (free) or 900 (toll) numbers allowing consumers to place an order from a catalog or advertisement.

Index:	Shows the relationship of two concepts numerically.
Insert or tip-in:	A pre-printed advertisement of one or more pages that is bound into a publication.
Kern:	Adjustment of space between two printed characters.
Key visual:	One frame that summarizes the main thrust of the commercial.
Layout:	An indication of what the finished print advertisement will look like.
Line extensions:	Additional products that bear the same brand name and offer the consumer varied options.
Mailing list:	Names of people held together by some kinship, such as subscribers to a magazine.
Makegood:	An advertisement run as a replacement for one that was scheduled but did not run, or ran incorrectly.
Market share:	The percentage held by one brand of all products sold in a category.
Mechanical (paste-up or camera-ready artwork):	The final assembly of the elements needed for the print advertisement to be produced.
Media:	Forms of communication that provide the public with news and entertainment, usually together with advertising.

Merge-purge:	When two or more mailing lists are combined or merged, duplicate names are weeded out.
Model release:	Legal form signed by a photographer's subject to permit reproduction of the likeness.
Objective:	The desired result of marketing efforts in business or advertising.
Off-peak hours:	Television viewing time that is less expensive than prime time.
On-air recall test:	A measure of commercial effectiveness based on asking viewers what they remember about a commercial they saw 24 hours previously.
Out of register:	If any one of the four-color printing plates is out of alignment, the color photograph they compose will be blurred.
Outbound:	Use of the telephone to sell a product or service or to close a sale previously made in a mailing or advertisement.
Penetration:	The proportion of persons (or homes) that are physically able to be exposed to a medium.
Personality:	Another term for brand image.
Persuasion testing:	A measure of commercial effectiveness based on measuring how the commercial will affect a consumer's

likelihood to buy the product or service.

Plate: A flat sheet used in printing and other reproduction processes.

POP (point of purchase): Display or other materials in-store.

Pop-up: Paper or other material cut to represent a visual, then folded flat and glued into the publication. When the reader reaches this page, the visual "pops up."

Positioning: The place held by a product or service in the consumer's mind.

Post analysis: Comparison of actual gross impressions delivered versus original estimates, after a media schedule has run.

Presenter: A spokesperson on camera.

Primary audience: Number of readers who get a publication at a newsstand or receive it as a subscriber at home. **Secondary** or **Passalong Audience** is the number of readers exposed to the publication other than by direct purchase.

Printing: There are four basic methods. **Letterpress,** in which the printing surface is raised and pressed against the paper. **Gravure,** in which the printing surface is depressed. **Lithography** (or **offset**): The image is first printed on a rubber roller or blanket, then offset onto the paper. **Screen** or **silk screen** uses a printing stencil.

Promise: A summary statement of the benefits of the product.

Promise testing: Research to identify the most important and meaningful benefit that can be offered by a product.

Proof: A printed version of an advertisement. The first one is a **repro proof,** pulled by hand from a reproduction proof press. Later come **color-corrected proofs.** The engraver runs **final proofs** on the publication stock.

PSA (public service announcement): A commercial for social or community causes broadcast by television stations at no cost.

Psychographics: Information such as values and lifestyles about a given group of the population.

Pulsing: Continuous advertising plus periodic bursts.

PUT: Percentage of people using television at any given time.

Quintile analysis: Used to evaluate the degree of impact of a media effort. Determined by dividing the number of people reached into five equal groups. The average frequency is computed for each subgroup.

Rating: Percentage of homes or individuals tuned in to the average quarter hour of a program.

Reach: Number of different persons who see or hear a message at least once. Also known as **cume**, **unduplicated** or **net** audience.

Redemption: Fulfillment of an offer, such as turning in coupons.

Rotoscoping: Film technique that combines animation with live action.

Rough cut: Early stage in the editing of a commercial.

Run-of-press (ROP): A print position request to run an advertisement anywhere in the publication.

Run-of-schedule (ROS): A broadcast position request to run a commercial at any time of day.

Sales promotion: A marketing technique to increase sales, usually through couponing, sweepstakes, contests, gifts or premiums, rebates, in-store displays.

SEC (Securities and Exchange Commission): Agency that regulates advertising for stocks and bonds.

Serif: A thin line that projects above and below certain letters.

SFX (sound effects): Sounds that are added after the commercial has been filmed.

Share: In broadcast, the audience of a program as a percentage of all households using the medium at the time.

Share-of-Voice (SOV): Number of times the audience sees or hears a brand's message in relation to all competitive messages.

Sheet: In out-of-home, a reference to the days when printing presses couldn't handle large sheets of paper. A **30-sheet board** now means a size, about 10 feet by 22 feet; no longer 30 sheets of paper.

Shooting board: Elaborate version of a storyboard which shows shot by shot what will be filmed or taped.

Shot: In film or tape, usually one scene.

Long shot: A scene that takes in the full view of the subject: A long shot of a person would show the entire body.

Medium shot: If of a person, the shot is from the waist up.

Close up (CU): Only the head.

Extreme close up (ECU): Only the eyes.

Showing: In outdoor and transit, the number of posters that can be seen by the adult population of one area in one day.

Simmons/MRI: Syndicated information that can be purchased about the buying and media habits of different population groups.

Slice-of-life: A commercial that uses a realistic situation and natural language to imitate real life.

Slotting allowance: Money paid by the manufacturer to the retailer—usually for a new product—to gain access to the computerized system and shelf space.

Snipe: Overlay to an existing billboard, usually to add information.

Sound design: Music, sound effects, background music—all elements of the sound track.

Spectaculars: Elaborate billboards that usually show more than the usual two-dimensional rectangle.

Split-run test:	Placing different versions of an advertisement in the same issue of one publication for testing.
Spot advertising:	Media purchased on a market-by-market basis.
Spread (double truck):	A print advertisement that takes up two facing pages.
Standard advertising unit (SAU):	A system of unit sizes in newspaper advertising.
Stock music:	Existing music that can be purchased for agreed-upon usage.
Stock photo:	Shot previously taken by a photographer that can be purchased for agreed upon usage.
Story appeal:	Something in the illustration of a print advertisement that makes the reader ask "what's going on here?"
Storyboard:	Drawings that depict the action of a commercial, together with a written description of what the viewer will see and hear.
Strategy:	A plan, preferably in writing, that charts the course of action for marketing your brand.
Support:	A reason for the consumer to believe your claim.
T-scope (tachistoscope):	Instrument that evaluates effectiveness of an advertisement, poster or

package by measuring eye movements.

Take-ones: Pads of tear-off blanks pasted on transit posters.

Target audience: Primary prospects sought by an advertiser.

Telemarketing: Use of the telephone to sell or buy.

Test marketing: Tracking the sales of a new or improved product in one or more cities before marketing it nationally.

Testimonial: A commercial that uses real people to endorse a product.

Tone and manner: A projection of your brand's image or personality.

Track: A component of the audio portion of any commercial. A **voice track,** with the actors' words, is combined with the **music track** and the **effects track** to make the final **soundtrack.**

Tracking studies: In-market research that constantly monitors one brand's performance against competition.

Trial-builders: A promotion aimed at generating purchase by new users.

True value concept: In direct marketing, the measurable, long-term value of each customer.

Typeface:	The style of type selected for the advertisement.
UPC scanning systems:	Universal product codes printed on products that reveal information when scanned electronically.
Uppercase and lowercase:	Capital letters as opposed to **lowercase** or small letters.
VALS (values and life-styles):	A syndicated system for sorting consumers into different life-style groups, and linking their behavior to their values.
VCR:	Videocassette recorder.
Verbatims:	The exact words used by people when asked to comment on rough or finished advertisements.
Video:	The written description on a storyboard of the visual flow of the commercial.
Viewers-per-Household (VPH):	Average number of persons watching or listening to a program in each home.
VO (Voice-over):	Indication on a storyboard that someone is speaking "off camera."
Weasels:	Wording in an advertisement that deliberately suggests the product does something it may not always do.
Zap:	Obliterating a commercial by fast-forwarding with a remote control device.

THE AUTHORS

KENNETH ROMAN is the former chairman and chief
executive of Ogilvy & Mather Worldwide.

JANE MAAS is chairman of Earle Palmer Brown/New York
and a former creative director of
Ogilvy & Mather, where the authors worked
together and wrote the first edition of this book.

Mr. Roman is also the coauthor (with Joel Raphaelson)
of *Writing that Works*. Mrs. Maas is also the author
of *Adventures of an Advertising Woman*
and *Better Brochures, Catalogs, and Mailing Pieces*.

Acknowledgments

The authors offer profound thanks to

Steve Arbeit, Keith Bantick, Luis Bassat, Drayton Bird, Max Blackston, John Blaney, Laura Bonington, Reg Brack, Sue Buck, Michael Buckland, Harold Burson, Ken Caffrey, Bill Chororos, Larry Cole, Jane Fitzgibbon, Sean Fitzpatrick, Richard Fowler, Mark Goldstein, Norman Goluskin, John Groman, Elaine Haller, Spencer Hapoienu, Rick Hatch, Sy Hinkes, Barbara Hughley, Ed Kleban, Meredith Layer, Doug Leeds, John Margaritis, Gil Maurer, Marianne Morvai, Julie Newton, Nick Nicholas, Faith Norwick, Tom Owen, Jerry Pickholz, Vel Richey-Rankin, Elaine Reiss, Russ Richmond, Joyce Rivas, Rob Smith, John Williams, Ruth Wooden, and Lester Wunderman, who contributed materials, thoughts, and comments for several chapters.

Alex Biel, Jules Fine, Anne Hastaba, Peter Larson, Toni Maloney, and Kent Mitchel, who reviewed the entire manuscript and improved it measurably.

Julian Bach, Tom Dunne, Robert Kalinowski, Michael Maas, and Ellen Roman, for their special support.

Book design by Barnett Design Group, Inc.

Photograph of Dr. Martin Luther King in The United Negro College Fund advertisement is used with the kind permission of the King estate.

Index

B

billboards, 54–58
Bird, Drayton, 59
brands
  brand equity, 2
  brand personality, 65,
    66, 95, 118–19
  consumer loyalty to, 1
  defined, 1–2
  do's and don't's, 8–10
  failure of, 8–10
  radio advertising of,
    53
brochures, 105
  artwork, 106–7
  copywriting, 107–8
  cover of, 106
  effectiveness, techniques
    for, 106–8
  envelope for, 108
  focus of, 106
  production costs,
    111–13
  travel, for, 108
  Burson, Howard,
    102

C

Calvin Klein, 47
campaigns
  attitude portrayed by, 74
  changing campaigns,
    77–78

elements of, 72–74, 78
examples of, 71
international
  advertising, 117–22
marketing principles
  and, 74–77
planning of, 75–77
promotions, 97–99
purpose of, 71
verbal elements, 73–74
visual elements, 72–73
catalogs
  artwork, 110–11
  copywriting, 110
  cover for, 109
  mailing lists, 111
  ordering from, 109–10
  production costs,
    111–13
celebrities as presenters,
  21–22
children, marketing to,
  132–35
clutter, 13–15, 87
Compaq, 67
comparative advertising,
  23–24
consumers
  legal protection for,
    137–42
  privacy versus market
    research, 142–43
copywriting, 43, 44–46
  brochures, 107–8
  catalogs, 110

campaigns, 97–99
case allowances, 93
cash refunds, 93
cents-off coupons, 93
contests, 94
displays, retails, *See*
displays
effectiveness, techniques
for, 96–99
new users, trial by,
96–97
pretesting of, 95–96
publicity, *See* public
relations
public relations, *See*
public relations
purpose of, 94
relationship marketing
and, 98–99
short-term incentives, 97
slotting allowances, 93
sponsorship of events,
94
sweepstakes, 94, 95
tracking results of, 96
trade deals, 93
publicity, *See* public
relations
public relations, 102, 104
news releases, 102–3
press kits, 102–3
special events, 103
sponsorships, 103
public service advertising,
142–45

Q

Q-Tips, 33
quality as selling point,
10–11

R

radio advertising
advantages of, 49–51
direct marketing, for,
68
effectiveness, techniques
for, 52–53
focus of ideas, 51
music, use of, 51–52
one-to-one
communication, 50, 51
promotions, use of, 53
Ralph Lauren, 74
relationship marketing
direct marketing, 67–
68
promotions, 98–99
repetition of ads, 82, 83,
84–86
research, *See* Market
research
retail, 42
promotions for, *See*
promotions
radio advertising for,
53
review boards, 141–42
Ryder trucks, 68, 69